# CREWE SHEDS

## Allan Baker & Gavin Morrison

LONDON

IAN ALLAN LTD

First published 1988

ISBN 0 7110 1809 X

Published by Ian Allan Ltd, Shepperton, Surrey; and printed by Ian Allan Printing Ltd at their works at Coombelands in Runnymede, England

Dedication:
Crewe Motive Power Men, Past, Present and Future.

Previous page:
**Rail House provides a panoramic view of Crewe Diesel Depot and holding sidings, with Classes 08, 25, 40 and 47 in evidence. In the background a Class 87-hauled down express passes the Carriage Shed. This scene was recorded on 7 September 1977.** *Barry J. Nicolle*

Front cover:
**'Royal Scot' No 46115 *Scots Guardsman* glints in the winter sunlight at Crewe North on 13 February 1965.** *Hugh Ballantyne*

Back cover, top:
**'Britannia' class 4-6-2 No 70044 stands near the coaling stage at Crewe North on the same day.** *Hugh Ballantyne*

Back cover, bottom:
**A view of Crewe South with the 70ft turntable in the foreground, taken on 14 January 1967.** *Martin Welch*

# Contents

# Preface

This book is the second joint effort by Gavin and myself, again a combination of his music and my words. It could justly be asked what our qualifications are to pen a book on Crewe's locomotive sheds, and in answering this question it has to be said that the blame falls fairly and squarely on my shoulders. An interest in railways and locomotives stems from as early an age as I can recall. Encouraged by my father, a keen and extremely accomplished model engineer, a railway career was a foregone conclusion. I had been driving miniature steam locomotives ever since I was old enough to be trusted with the regulator, and watching trains at every opportunity. Indeed, it was my father who first used to take me to Crewe on Saturday mornings and these visits were the prelude to many happy hours spent there. Studying locomotives going on and off the North Shed was a grand preoccupation, but only once did I manage to penetrate the depths of this hallowed place, and little did I think that one day it would be within my grasp!

Largely thanks to Geoff Sands, whom I mention at length later in this book, I decided to begin my career as an apprentice in the Motive Power Department, rather than going for a similar career in the main workshops, or on the footplate — the latter my original leaning. Equally, it was Geoff who suggested that I go to the larger sheds at Crewe, rather than my native Stoke-on-Trent. I have looked back on neither of these two decisions since, except with the complete satisfaction of knowing that, at the tender age of but 15 years, I made the right choice, and one which has stood me in good stead from that day to this.

I commenced a six-year apprenticeship within the Motive Power Department, initially at Crewe North Shed, and went to work on and about locomotives at that hallowed domain of my wildest dreams. During the years that were to follow, many were the changes, eventually including the complete closure of the North Shed, and its subsequent demolition. I recall many of my workmates saying 'They will never close the North Shed' — and so it seemed, but they did! However, I enjoyed it all, and when asked 'Where did you start?' take pride in telling colleagues 'Crewe North Motive Power Depot'.

I consider myself very fortunate to have been able to spend time at Crewe North when it was still going just about full blast with steam locomotives; we had diesels, but the place only really started to run down its steam activity a year or so after I started. It was a tremendous place, and I shall never forget my experiences on steam locomotive maintenance and repair; I treasure these memories, and consider myself very lucky to have been able to be so involved with the everyday operation of steam locomotives at grass-roots level. To have done so at the largest passenger locomotive depot on the London Midland Region, and one of the most famous sheds of all time, was an added bonus. As a link with the past, I worked with fitters who remembered shaping wooden brake blocks with an adze, to fit the circumference of the tyres.

It would have been nice, with this book, to have emulated Peter Townend's classic history of the King's Cross locomotive depots, so well chronicled in his splendid book *Top Shed*. But this volume is by no means such an erudite treatise, and no more is it intended to be. Rather, here I have collected together the broad history, so far as information is to hand and I am able, and within the constraints of size, of the Crewe locomotive depots. I have concentrated more on the North and South steam sheds, and the steam era generally, because I think most of my readers will find this more interesting, and because there will be folk aplenty in the future to deal with later events. Nevertheless there are chapters on the diesel and electric depots, the former in slightly more detail, both because I know it better, and because it has gone through more changes.

I will, no doubt, be accused of bias towards my own experiences in this book, and this will be fair criticism, so you have here very much a Crewe book about Allan Baker, rather than an Allan Baker book about Crewe! It is, therefore, doubtful if the historian in search of facts about when locomotive number so and so was allocated to Crewe North, or what diagrams the 'Royal Scots' worked in 1930, or when some minor shed extension was built, will find what he is looking for within these pages. What the more general reader will find, however, is much local lore, reminiscence and something of the activities of the men and their locomotives. However, it has to be said that I have tried to cover the historical aspects as well as I am able, and I must take the blame for any errors or omissions a diligent reader might detect. Of course, any such further information will be very welcome. It must also be added that any opinions stated are entirely my own, and should not be taken as official views in any context.

I mention on another page that when I commenced work at Crewe, how different I found the people there to those of my native North Staffordshire, but since leaving Crewe in 1974 (and having subsequently worked on three of the remaining four BR Regions, or four of five if one includes the new Anglia Region!) I look back on my days there with affection. We had some wonderful times, and they were a splendid group of workmates, many of whom I still take pride in calling my friends.

Gavin has very largely been responsible for selection of the photographs, and in doing so has tried not only to illustrate all the points I raise in my writings, but also to portray something of what Crewe and its locomotives were all about. I think he has been very largely successful, but if the occasional photograph can be criticised for its technical merit, then it has been included because it illustrates some point we have been otherwise unable to portray. One would have expected to be able to locate photographs galore of Crewe and its sheds, showing just about every conceivable locomotive, and from every conceivable angle, but it is surprising how difficult it has been to approach this goal. Equally, the drawings and diagrams have all been selected to show points raised in the text, and we owe a great debt to many people for their extreme generosity in allowing us to use their work and researches in this respect. All are, we hope, duly

Above:
**'Royal Scot' class 4-6-0 No 46154 pauses at Crewe adjacent to one of its intended replacements, a Class AL3 (later 83) electric locomotive.**
*The Late Brian Haresnape*

# Acknowledgements

There is no pleasanter task for an author than to sit down at his desk when the pressure of completing to a publisher's deadline is over, and pen a few lines of acknowledgement to all those who have helped him in his task. It provides time for reflection, as one recalls all the help and assistance so willingly given and the pleasure of opening some eagerly awaited package of photographs or whatever. My pleasure in compiling this book has been enhanced in being able to recall, research and write about so much that I value — not least all my workmates of so many years ago. A number of visits to Crewe in recent months, and after a gap of several years, have provided some fascinating, absorbing and memorable hours. It has also enabled me to answer some outstanding queries that have been 'bugging' me for years!

For information I have to thank especially Roger Griffiths, John Hooper (who also kindly did some proof reading), Chris Hawkins and George Reeve, all keen members of The Engine Shed Society, for allowing me, without any reservations, to use the results of their researches; all are experts in their own right, and authors of standard works on locomotive sheds. David Patrick and Nick Piggott assisted in this sphere too.

Peter Rowledge was the Shedmaster at Crewe Diesel Depot during my first period there, and we have remained firm friends ever since. We constantly find each other of valued assistance in our respective spheres of railway historical research. Fred West was the first, last and indeed only (his words!) Depot Superintendent at Crewe, as well as being the first Area Maintenance Engineer, and it was he and Doug Fisher (his Assistant at the Diesel Depot) who presided over my first steps on the promotional ladder. Both Peter and Fred spent several periods of their careers at Crewe, and their recollections have been of much assistance in clearing up all number of points. Likewise Neville Davies, as well as having the foresight to take photographs on Crewe North, appointed

mentioned in the acknowledgements, and our gratitude is no less sincere for having to consign them there.

It would be remiss of both Gavin and myself if we did not pay a tribute here to Margaret and Angela. What wonderful and considerate ladies we both have the pleasure of partnering: lonely is their vigil as we spend hours in darkrooms and studies! Angela bore the added burden of typing, processing and very often editing the text. Last, but by no means least, it has been enjoyable to work with Gavin on a joint book again, and especially in my case to recall and write about so much of what I hold dear. We can only hope that our readers get just something of the pleasure and enjoyment from this volume as we have had in compiling it; because if this is so, we will consider our efforts justly rewarded.

In my office I have what I refer to as my 'roll of honour', locomotive shed plates from the depots I have worked at, and mounted on a board. When I feel in need of inspiration, am having a rough time, or perhaps need a little patience in dealing with some matter related to the busy world we live in today, I pause for a moment and look up at them, and especially the one at the top bearing the code 5A. Thereafter, the memories of Crewe North, its men and its engines come flooding back, and they never leave me without a clear path in my mind as to what I should do next . . .

# Introduction

Crewe: what thoughts and memories the name conjures up in any railway enthusiast's mind, and few cannot have visited the place at one time or another. Indeed, there can be few travellers who have used our railways, and will not have memories of passing through — or perhaps, more likely, changing trains at this most famous railway junction. It is surprising, therefore, that so little has been written about Crewe as a railway junction. True, there is an excellent social and economic history of the town, and its involvement with the railway companies, and it would be difficult to better W. H. Chaloner's erudite and definitive effort in this sphere. Likewise, there is an excellent history of the locomotive workshops, in their day the largest and most independent such establishment in the world, and the late and lamented Brian Reed's book is a model of its kind. But, try as one might, the reader will find little written on the history of the station, junctions, marshalling yards, locomotive sheds and the like. Scattered articles he will find aplenty, chapters in general histories of the London & North Western Railway (LNWR) and many illustrations all over the place; but gathered together in book form, he will look for in vain. One could have expected the recent 150-year celebrations of Crewe's me to my first supervisory position, and our professional paths have continued to cross frequently ever since. Jack Hollick and Derek Barrie have helped me with details of the history of the GWR route between Nantwich and Wellington.

On the photographic front, many people have helped Gavin and I to present so wide a coverage, freely and willingly delving into their collections to find all number of useful views. Special thanks for searching their achives, therefore, go to: Alan Bridges, Dave Donkin, Bruce Ellis (for access to his father's collection, the late A. G. Ellis), Mike Fell, Michael Mensing, Brian Morrison, Tim Shuttleworth, Martin Welch and the late George Wheeler. George was a tremendous character, whom I came to know well long after his Crewe North activities, despite my being there for some of the period, and he was always extremely generous to me with copies of his work. I thank his wife and son Stephen for allowing us to use his magnificent Pacific portraits on Crewe North. As for so many of us, they were George's favourite locomotives.

For maps and plans, I have to thank an ever-tolerant Mrs J. M. Williams of the Cheshire Record Office, who put up with my unlimited requests for copies of maps, my old friend and co-author of other works Allen Civil, for redrawing an old plan of the GWR shed at Gresty Lane, and Chris Preston who managed to dig out many old plans from the archives of the Area Civil Engineer at Crewe. Of course, I thank British Railways for being able to use them, along with the official photographs.

Last, I would like to thank Crewe Motive Power men past and present, including Bill Davies, Brian Heath, Harry Newbiggin, Ray Metcalfe, Ken Parker, the late George Preece and John Skellon. I could go on with many many more names, but lack of space must intervene. However, I want to single out especially Geoff Oliver, a fitter at the Diesel Depot now, and I write in complete confidence that none of his colleagues past or present, will begrudge my picking out Geoff to represent them all. Geoff started as an apprentice at the North Shed in January 1943, as I myself was to do 18 years later, and apart from a few years at Longsight in 1950-53, has been at Crewe all his career, and for many years in the breakdown gang too. Of all the fitters I worked with during my apprenticeship, and I worked with some smashing guys, I enjoyed my time with Geoff most, and we worked together quite a lot. He was an excellent tradesman, who taught me a lot, including many tricks of the trade, could have been a supervisor many times over had he wanted, and I can think of no better person to represent Crewe Motive Power men, to all of whom Gavin and I have dedicated this volume.

Allan C. Baker
Great Totham
Essex
January 1988

association with railways to have brought forth something, but it has not been the case.

This book is an attempt to help redress the balance, and in the space available I have gathered together as much as I am able, on the history of Crewe's locomotive sheds. These establishments were far smaller than the Works, but no less important to the everyday operation of a railway and, as can be expected during their long history, there were several different sheds, and many alterations to them. Crewe is perhaps unique, certainly outside London, in that one of the pre-grouping railway companies found it necessary to maintain two locomotive sheds which were completely independent, save in their management, and within one mile of each other. The sheds were also two of the LNWR's largest, and this gives some idea of the amount of railway activity at Crewe in its heyday. In those days over 300 locomotives were allocated to the two sheds, and around 1,500 footplatemen were employed. Even today, it is impossible to walk the streets of Crewe, at any time of the day or night, on any day of the week, without seeing a footplateman going to or from his work.

After the opening of the new shed south of the station in 1897, which thereafter assumed the responsibility for the goods locomotives, the North Shed became a passenger depot, and the largest locomotive depot on the LNWR, and later the largest passenger depot on the London Midland & Scottish Railway (LMS). But Crewe North was more than just the largest, it was the most prestigious locomotive depot on the old LNWR and later on the LMS, and can justifiably lay claim to have been the most famous on the whole of British Railways. True, it can be argued that such claims to fame are dependent on the beholder's point of view, but by any criterion, the North Shed stands high.

Almost all the major locomotive achievements on the West Coast main line feature North Shed engines and men. In the Railway Races to the north of 1888 and 1895, Crewe engines and men achieved the finest results, and broke all the records; and, moreover, on the toughest section of either route, between Preston and Carlisle. It was the legendary combination of Driver 'Big Ben' Robinson and Fireman W. Wolstencroft, with the locomotive *Hardwicke*, all from Crewe, that made the record-breaking 141-mile run from Crewe to Carlisle in 126min on that truly historic last night of the 1895 Races. Their average speed between Preston and Carlisle was 67.5mph, and all this achieved by a locomotive weighing no more than 32 tons! Little wonder the authorities did not have the heart to scrap little *Hardwicke* when its days were done, and it lives on as a permanent reminder of that night, and of the men who drove and maintained the locomotive.

'Claughton' No 1159 *Ralph Brocklebank* was a Crewe North engine, manned by Crewe North men, when it made its epic dynamometer car test run between Crewe and Carlisle in November 1913, and achieved an indicated horse power of no less than 1,669 on Shap, and a drawbar pull of 9⅞ tons on Grayrigg. This was the highest power output ever recorded

by a British steam locomotive up to that time, Swindon products included, I hasten to add! Like all members of the class, 1159 was built at Crewe.

In November 1936 Crewe North Driver Tom Clarke, with Firemen C. Fleet and A. Shaw, took the 'Princess Royal' class Pacific No 6201 *Princess Elizabeth* on her high speed run prior to the introduction of the fast 'Coronation Scot' nonstop train between Euston and Glasgow. This through working with the 'Princess' had to be with Crewe men, because at that time they alone had the route knowledge of the complete West Coast main line. These stalwarts completed the northbound journey of 401.4 miles in 353.38min, at an average speed of 66.1mph, returning south the following day in 344.15min, at an average speed of exactly 70mph. It was Tom Clarke again, this time with Fireman John Lewis, who took 'Big Lizzie' No 6220 *Coronation* on its record-breaking stint down Madeley Bank when a speed of 114mph was reached, a world record at that time, on a press run prior to the introduction of the new 'Coronation Scot' train on 29 June 1937.

I could go on, but will conclude by recording that again it was Crewe North men, in the shape of Driver C. Garrett and Fireman S. Farrington, who took No 6234 *Duchess of Aber-*

*corn* on the first leg of its record-breaking run between Crewe and Glasgow, in February 1939. It was during this high power test run, on the return climb to Shap with the North Shed men again in charge, that the highest drawbar horsepower ever recorded by a steam locomotive in this country was achieved — 2,511.

Below:
**A superb portrait of Pacific No 46232 *Duchess of Montrose*, in excellent external condition, and seemingly ready to leave the shed with safety valves lifting. It stands on No 2 road of the Middle Shed, on 20 August 1955, and the 66A shed plate indicates its 'home' shed is Glasgow Polmadie, and this particular locomotive spent no less than 22 out of its 24 years of working life from that shed and, like the other long-term Polmadie residents, managed to accrue a lower annual mileage than the English-based members of the class. Likewise, Polmadie engines were painted green, after the decision had been taken to paint some members of the class in LMS maroon, because they predominantly worked night trains. Notice the foreshortened Nos 1 and 2 roads, thus allowing space at the end of the shed for the canteen, the rear wall of which can just be seen behind the engine. The poor state of the roof is apparent even by this date, and the stored arch bricks to the left are worthy of note. As the breakdown crane is not standing on No 1 road, it must have been out on a job when this photograph was taken.** *Brian Morrison*

Above:
**A general view of the eastern end of the Electric Traction Depot, taken shortly after opening, in around 1961. To the left of the main building can be seen the administration and workshop block, and on the extreme right behind the overhead line stanchion, can just be discerned the platform and coaches of the Works train. The two locomotives to the left with the sheets over them, appear to have had their main transformers removed, possibly for some form of rectification under guarantee arrangements, as they are almost new. The depot stands on the site of the former Carriage Works Yard, the actual Works site being to the right.** *British Railways No D4468*

Crewe North men can justifiably claim to have worked the toughest footplate job ever regularly assigned in this country, for they worked the mighty sleeping car and mail trains between Crewe and Perth — which were double-home jobs — two trains each way every night, 296 miles and with around 600 tons behind the tender. That this could be achieved night in and night out was in no small measure because the locomotives were kept in first class condition by the maintenance staff, and with these and other achievements, Crewe North can fairly claim to have been the premier locomotive shed on the 'Premier Line', not only in LNWR days, but subsequently under LMS and BR auspices too. Doubtless, this statement will bring forth many critics but I stand by what I say!

Between 1960 and 1963 there were no less than five locomotive depots at Crewe; the North and the South steam sheds, the former Great Western Railway (GWR) establishment at Gresty Lane, and the newer diesel and electric depots — it was a haven for train spotters! Despite being a native of the nearby Pottery towns, much of my train spotting was spent at Crewe, at the north end of Platforms 3 and 4; what a splendid place it was on a Saturday in the summer. Here then is my story of Crewe, its locomotive depots, their locomotives and, equally significantly, the men.

Above left:
**Interior view of the Diesel Depot taken during November 1957, shortly after opening, and obviously posed. Looking north with No 1 road to the right and the workshop area to the extreme left, the three diesel railcar sets are a Derby Lightweight two-car set on the right, and two Birmingham Railway Carriage & Wagon (BRCW) three-car sets to the left, all being used on the local services at this period.** *British Railways No M2166*

Left:
**'Britannia' Pacific No 70051 *Firth of Forth*, taking an apparent overdose of water and standing adjacent to the coaling plant at Crewe South on 4 March 1967; notice the lattice steel wagon hoist and the reinforced concrete coal bunker. This view looks north.** *Dave Donkin*

9

# 1 Crewe

There has been much speculation over the years as to why the Grand Junction Railway (GJR) built its locomotive and carriage workshops at Crewe, thus pre-empting the creation of what became possibly the largest, certainly the most railway-dominated, and no doubt the best known of Britain's 'railway towns'. Nowhere else did the railway quite achieve such control over almost everything, as it was to do at Crewe. The town came to house not only the largest railway workshops in the country, if not the world, but also extensive marshalling yards, locomotive sheds and came to be the junction of lines radiating to Shrewsbury, Stoke-on-Trent, Holyhead and Manchester, along with the trunk route between London and the north.

At Crewe the railway company supplied the town with its water and

gas, and later built for it one of the finest municipal parks in the country. Indeed, in Crewe the LNWR — at the time of the grouping the largest joint stock company operating a railway anywhere in the world — was Crewe; the town existed for the railway.

The GJR was incorporated by Act of Parliament, The Grand Junction Railway Act 1835 (Wm IV 3-4 Ch xxxiv), which received the Royal Assent on 6 May 1833. This Act empowered the company to build a line between Newton-le-Willows, just north of Warrington, and Birmingham; construction commenced on 22 May that year in the Weaver valley. The 78-mile-long line was opened in its entirety and for passenger traffic on 4 July 1837, goods traffic following in February of the next year. This line, which was one of the first trunk routes in the country, came to pass

through the very small hamlet of Crewe, in the Cheshire parish of Church Coppenhall, 53 miles from Birmingham.

Like many of the early trunk routes the GJR was laid out with little thought for intermediate traffic, being primarily intended to provide a through route between Liverpool — reached via the Liverpool & Manchester Railway (L&MR), with which it made a junction at Newton-le-

Below:
**A fascinating picture taken at the north end of Crewe station on the through roads, showing the unique BR Standard Class 8 Pacific No 71000 *Duke of Gloucester*, which was fitted with Caprotti valve gear, and BTH Class AL1 (later Class 81) electric locomotive No E3007; which appears to be virtually new. No 71000 was a Crewe North engine for all its short service life of eight years.** *The late Brian Haresnape*

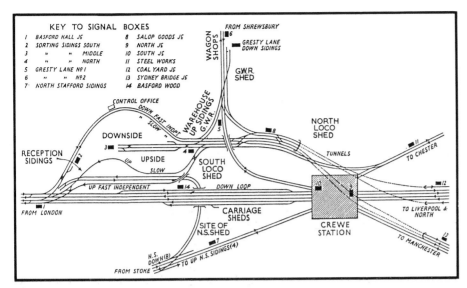

Willows — and Birmingham. Therefore, in Cheshire, it took a path midway between the industrial areas of Northwich, Middlewich and Sandbach to the east, and the market town of Nantwich to the west. Likewise, it missed the Pottery towns centred around Stoke-on-Trent and Newcastle-under-Lyme, and only the Staffordshire county town seems to have been favoured with direct access! Some 26 miles north of Stafford the line passed through Church Coppenhall, which was itself 1½ miles north of where the line crossed the Nantwich to Wheelock Turnpike road (Turnpiked by Act of Parliament dated 1816), a road which also gave access to Manchester; at Church Coppenhall a small wayside station was built.

A short distance to the east of where the Turnpike road crossed the railway lay Crewe Hall, the extensive and beautiful mansion and estate of the Earl of Crewe. Doubtless due to these factors — the Crewe Estate and the Turnpike Road — a station was opened where road and railway crossed, seemingly only a few months after the line opened, and it assumed the name Crewe. Church Coppenhall station did not last very long and closed, apparently due to lack of patronage, in September 1840.

By 1839 there was an engine shed at Crewe, just north of the road bridge and south of the then projected junction with the Chester & Crewe Railway on an area of land known as Horse Pasture. The Chester & Crewe Railway had been incorporated in 1837, the year the GJR opened, and the Chester & Crewe Railway Act (Vic 1 Ch lxiii) had received the Royal Assent on 30 July that year. This Act gave powers to build a railway, 21 miles long, between Chester — the

Below:
**The up 'Welshman' is loaded to 15 or 16 coaches as it leaves from the south end of the station headed by Camden-based unrebuilt 'Royal Scot' No 46140 The King's Royal Rifle Corps, in around 1950-51. Notice the tortuous passage from No 3 platform to the up fast line. A classic and unmistakable Treacy portrait.** *The late Eric Treacy*

county town — and Crewe, where it would join with the GJR. Thus, as can be seen, from an early date Crewe was to be a junction.

Unfortunately, the Chester & Crewe company fell into financial difficulties very soon, being unable to raise the necessary capital to construct its line, and it was bailed out by absorption into the GJR as soon as 1839; the line was opened on 1 October 1840. Very soon afterwards another line was projected, in this case to link Manchester to the expanding railway system, and although it had originally been intended to build a separate line all the way to Birmingham, in the event a junction was made with the GJR at Crewe. So it came about that the rather grandiosely titled Manchester & Birmingham Railway, incorporated by Act of Parliament dated 30 July 1837 — The Manchester & Birmingham Railway Act (Vic 1 Ch lxviv) — built just 30¾ miles of railway, which opened throughout on 10 August 1842.

However, Crewe's small single-road engine shed was not built because of these projected traffic increases, but to house the banking engines needed for the ascent south of Crewe towards Madeley, which came to be called Madeley Bank. This incline of nearly 10 miles included a 3½-mile section of 1 in 177, the remainder averaging 1 in 303; not very steep or long by later standards, but sufficient to cause concern and restrict loads with the motive power then available. Indeed, over the years this climb has taxed many a more modern locomotive, either heavily loaded or, perhaps, starting cold from Crewe. There was another small shed at Madeley, used for servicing the engines before they returned to Crewe.

Although out of strict chronological order, it is perhaps opportune at this point to continue the story of Crewe as a junction, seeing its completion as such with the opening of other lines. The GJR did itself have plans to serve north Staffordshire, with its rich industrial wealth and its thriving pottery industry, by a branch from Crewe. However, in the event this link was built by the independent North Staffordshire Railway (NSR), and this company opened its 14½-mile line between Crewe and Stoke via Kidsgrove on 9 October 1848. This intrepid little company was the only one to invade the LNWR monopoly at Crewe with a direct line and, despite many attempts, it never did fall into

the LNWR net, remaining independent until the 1923 grouping. Last but by no means least, the Shrewsbury & Crewe line received the Royal Assent on 20 August 1853 (Vic 17 Ch ccxvi), and the 33-mile section was opened on 1 September 1858. The long delay between authorisation and opening was due to differences of opinion regarding the site of the station at Shrewsbury — this was a joint arrangement with the GWR, hence the delay!

With the completion of the line to Shrewsbury, Crewe as a junction was complete, and so it remains to this day. However, a couple more lines are worthy of mention. First, in 1861 the Nantwich & Market Drayton Railway was incorporated and authorised to build a line from Nantwich, which was 4½ miles from Crewe on the Shrewsbury line, 10¾ miles due south to the Shropshire border market town of Market Drayton. This railway was operated from its opening on 19 October 1863 by the GWR, despite being completely isolated from it. Later, the Wellington &

Top:
**Unnamed 'Claughton' No 23, in unlined plain black livery, makes a fine sight as it comes off the Chester line, and across the North Junction. Notice the Crewe North Junction signalbox, and the 'Spider Bridge' connection between works and station. This bridge carried the 18in gauge internal works railway. A 'George the Fifth' Class 4-4-0 stands on the right.** *Ian Allan Library*

Above:
**One of the handsome Stanier 2-6-0 Moguls, No 42962, approaching the station at the head of a lengthy freight off the Chester line on 19 August 1955. These locomotives were to be seen around Crewe during all of the 30 years of their working lives, being mainly allocated in the Birkenhead and Chester areas, as well as at some of the Birmingham depots. From left to right note: North Shed Yard, Old Works, Crewe North Junction signalbox and, immediately behind it, the works clock tower. To the right of the signalbox is the former No 1 Erecting Shop — one-time 'engine in steam shed' — and then, continuing right, the main line north, Grease Works and Manchester line. The platform face to the left is No 3, and as the train is not taking the Independent lines, it must be destined for the North Stafford route to Stoke.** *Brian Morrison*

Above:
**Many readers of this book will recognise this photograph more than any other, and it will probably bring back happy memories of hours spent standing on the bridge at the north end of the station. From here could be observed everything that passed, including that on the Independent goods avoiding lines. Motor fitted Ivatt 2-6-2T No 41229, allocated to the North Shed for just about all its life is ready to leave Platform 3A at the north end of the station, with the 12.38 to Northwich, on 20 August, 1955. Notice the modernisation work already underway, which eventually saw demolition of this bridge.**
*Brian Morrison*

Right:
**A fine night study of one of the station pilots, on this occasion No 47521, provided by the South Shed, and going about its nocturnal duties on 8 July 1966, standing on the release road between Platforms 1A and 2A. The engine carries the standard headlamp code for the Crewe station pilots, a red light over one buffer, and a white one over the other.** *The late Paul Riley*

Left:
**Aerial view of Basford Hall Marshalling Yards, looking northeast, with the South Shed and yard to the top left. Notice that on this date, 22 April 1954, the westernmost four roads are roofless, but some remedial work seems to have been carried out on the surviving sections of the roof — observe parts in a lighter colour. The 70ft turntable is just off the extreme top left-hand corner, and below it can be seen the Tranship Warehouse. To the right of the South Shed, on the opposite side of the main line, can be seen the Carriage Sheds, and the line running across the top right of the picture, is the former North Stafford line to Stoke. The site of the former NSR shed was just to the rear of the North Stafford Sidings signalbox, itself just discernible, centre left. Notice the curving connection between the NSR line and Marshalling Yards, which passes under the main line south; left of this bridge can be seen the concrete bases of the oil storage tanks, installed during the abortive postwar plans to convert many locomotives to oil firing. To the right centre can be seen the Independent 'engine line', crossing over the NSR connection, and providing direct access for locomotives between Basford Hall South and the South Shed. The Independent goods lines themselves, can be seen skirting the marshalling yards to left and right.**
*Hunting Aerofilms A53946*

Below left:
**Another aerial view of Crewe, looking north in 1947. The station is to the bottom right, and the Crewe Arms Hotel can be seen to its right. This photograph provides a fine panoramic view of the North Shed and yard, along with the streets surrounding it, and the many terraced houses built by the railway company to house its employees. From the right can be seen the Middle Shed, with its three hipped roof sections intact, and minus smoke vents, indicating its use for engines undergoing repairs and maintenance. Next comes Abba, with the shortened westernmost section, known as the Cage, and the Queens Hotel clearly visible; smoke vents on this shed illustrate its predominant use for engines in steam. Notice between Abba and the next building, the Stock Shed, the two uncovered roads used in connection with the coaling plant, and where lurked The Ghost of Abyssinia. The coaling plant itself, can be seen as the centre of much activity in the yard. By this date much of the Stock Shed roof had been demolished, and little use seems to be being made of its roads, apart from some coal wagon storage. Notice the turntable just north of the coaling plant, and the Old Works beyond, with the former No 1 erecting shop alongside the main line north. Crewe North Junction is in the centre of the photograph, with the Grease Works and race track in the apex formed by the main line and the Manchester line. The buildings immediately south of the Middle Shed housed the Outdoor Machinery Department. Notice the Independent goods lines burrowing under the North Junction.**
*Hunting Aerofilms A13316*

Drayton Railway, incorporated 1862, extended the line 15½ miles south to Wellington, thereby forming a junction with the main GWR system; this section opened on 16 October 1867. Both these lines, as might be expected, were eventually absorbed by the GWR: the Wellington & Drayton Railway on 30 July 1866, and the Nantwich & Market Drayton on 1 July 1897. It was by this line, from Wellington to Nantwich, that the GWR later obtained running powers over the LNWR between Nantwich and Crewe, and it eventually built its own locomotive shed at Crewe, situated at Gresty Lane which opened in 1870. Secondly, the direct line to Liverpool, leaving the GJR main line north of Crewe at Weaver Junction, was completed 1 April 1869, and thus obviated Liverpool trains having to go by the circuitous route via Warrington and Newton-le-Willows.

Originally, the GJR built its locomotives, carriages and wagons, and had repair workshops alongside those of the L&MR at Edge Hill, Liverpool. This may have been economical, but it was 15 miles away from the nearest point on the GJR, although the GJR did have running powers over the L&MR between Newton-le-Willows and Liverpool, and these were exercised daily. Despite the obvious difficulties, these workshops seem to have sufficed until 1840, by which time they were becoming a constant headache to everyday operations, due both to their location and limited size. Something had to be done. In view of the

developments at Crewe in terms of junction facilities, along with its central position on the main line as well as the availability of land there, the directors decided to make Crewe the site of their new workshops.

It would seem that Joseph Locke, the GJR Engineer, was much in favour of this move and may have been instrumental in tipping the scales with the directors in their choice of Crewe. By June 1840 land was being purchased for the new workshops, and Locke was being asked by his directors to prepare plans and estimates.

Crewe Locomotive Works was first opened in the spring of 1843, along with the nucleus of the town that was to house the workers and their families. Thus was started the sequence of events that, with extension after extension, gave the Works a surface area of 148 acres by 1900, and found work for over 8,000 employees. Here, locomotives and rolling stock were built with the bare minimum of bought in components, and of all the railway-owned workshops in the British Isles, Crewe alone made its own steel — and it was not just locomotives and rolling stock

Below:
**A typical row of railway-built terraced houses, looking east along Richard Moon Street in Hightown Crewe, on 27 February 1988. At the far end can be seen the Technical College — dating from 1897 — and beyond it Flag Lane. Richard Moon (later Sir Richard) was Chairman of the LNWR from 1861 to 1891.** *Gavin Morrison*

that were built there, but much else, ranging from the railway lines themselves, to signals, platelayers' huts and office furniture.

The town grew with the workshops: in 1831 the township of Monks Coppenhall and Crewe had a total population of 148 people; by 1851 it had risen to 4,571; in 1861 it totalled 8,159; and by 1871 reached no less than 17,810. In the inter-war period it peaked at 46,497 in 1921.

By Act of Parliament dated 16 July 1846 (Vic 9-10 Ch civ), the GJR, together with the London & Birmingham Railway and the Manchester & Birmingham Railway, amalgamated to form the LNWR — the L&MR having amalgamated with the GJR the previous year. The LNWR was to dominate the destiny of Crewe for the following 77 years, until it too was swallowed up and became a constituent of the LMS, under the provisions of the 1921 Railways Act on 1 January 1923.

*Left:*
**Taken on 4 April 1985 from Platform 1, and looking north, this view shows Crewe Station 'A' Cabin. The station offices are to the extreme right, and Platform 1 formed a part of the second of the two additional island platforms, this one being built in the 1896-1904 remodelling.** *L. A. Nixon*

*Centre left:*
**The second of the 15 Class AL3s (later Class 83s) built at Vulcan Foundry in 1960, No E3025 (later No 83002) stands on No 4 platform engine release road, with an unidentified AL6 (later Class 86); both are awaiting their next turns of duty around 1966.**
*The Late Eric Treacy*

*Bottom left:*
**Ex-LMS Class 4 tank No 42590 stands at the north end of Platform 5, with the through coaches to Bristol and Plymouth, which would have arrived from Glasgow earlier in the day, at the rear of the morning Glasgow to Birmingham train. They are waiting to be attached to the afternoon Manchester to Plymouth train, which would shortly arrive, via the crossover road seen in the distance, from the 'up through' to Platform 5. Notice the Crewe Arms Hotel to left, and the new bridge carrying the Nantwich Road over the station. Around 1959.** *T. Lewis*

Right:
**'Royal Scot' No 46164, *The Artist's Rifleman*,** leaves Crewe on 19 August 1955, at the head of a down Ocean Liner Express, 'The Empress Voyager'. Despite only going to Liverpool, the locomotive would appear to have come on to the train at Crewe, judging by the tender full of coal, although as the train is leaving from one of the through roads, it would not have called for passenger purposes. Notice the old station buildings on the road bridge above, and the Coffee Tavern on Platform 3 to left. *Brian Morrison*

Centre right:
**On 1 June 1985, the eve of the Crewe remodelling, Class 85 No 85005 passes through Crewe with the down 'Manchester Pullman'. By this date, the use of these locomotives on such prestigious workings was rare indeed.** *Gavin Morrison*

Below:
**An up Freightliner passes Crewe South Junction signalbox on 22 October 1983, headed by Class 86/0 No 86005. This sub-class of locomotive was intended for freight traffic, being equipped for multiple-unit operation. The signalbox dates from the 1938 resignalling of Crewe, itself being replaced — although it still stands — during the 1985 remodelling. The older box was exactly opposite this one, just off the picture to the left, and its brick base is still standing.** *Gavin Morrison*

17

Right:
**Class 86/2 No 86256 *Pebble Mill* stands at the north end of Platform 1 with a down express on 18 September 1982, as the staff sort out the mail. On the right are the Independent lines to Chester, with the Manchester and Preston Independent lines further right, and in the cutting. Observe, just to the right of the locomotive, the remains of the foundations for an old water column.**
*Gavin Morrison*

Centre right:
**LNWR 4-6-0 'Claughton' class No 1019 *Columbus*, one of the 1917 batch which were turned out in plain black livery, and seen here leaving Platform 4 for the south, shortly after the end of World War 1. Notice the large water tank above the engine, used to supply locomotive needs. No 1019 was a Crewe North engine from new, and in view of its tender full of coal, would have come on to the train at Crewe.**
*Ian Allan Library*

Below:
**The Crewe Arms Hotel, originally built by the LNWR in 1880, seen here on 27 February 1988. The building, as well as being a fine piece of period architecture, is adjacent to the station, and a notable landmark on any photograph of the station area.**
*Gavin Morrison*

# 2
# North Shed

There is a suggestion that the former No 1 Erecting Shop, which was one of the first parts of the Old Works, had originally been used as an engine shed. There were four roads in this 1843-built 196ft × 80ft building, which finally ceased to be used as an erecting shop after the 1926 westward extensions to the works area, notably with the completion of the No 10 Erecting Shop. It became instead a boiler and general plate store. Immediately to the north of this shop, and contiguous with it, the No 2 erecting shop became the main boiler shop at the same time, with Nos 3, 4 and 5 Erecting Shops (which were at

right angles to, and north of the No 2 Shop) taking over the remainder of the boiler work for the whole works. This was all part of a large reorganisation of the workshops about this time, and thereafter all locomotive boiler construction for the whole of the LMS was undertaken at Crewe.

This building is sometimes referred to as the 'engine in steam shed', but I think this has to be read in the context of locomotives in steam coming in for repairs, rather than servicing. Clearly, in the early days, with so much expertise within the Works, there would be a tendency to send locomotives there for repairs, whereas in

other places, the staff on hand would perhaps have had to manage with their own resources. Doubtless therefore, the shop got this name because the 'running' people, who all came under the same ultimate chief, sent the odd engine in for some repair or adjustment, rather than for the conventional shed duties of servicing and fuelling between trips. Of course, as the number of locomotives requiring attention at Crewe increased, it became less and less practical to disrupt the erecting shop with such minor repairs, and the sheds had to become more self-sufficient.

Latterly the works shunting locomotives were maintained and repaired inside an 1853-54 southwards extension of the old No 1 Erecting Shop, with the two roads nearest the main line being utilised for about two engine lengths inside the shop. So whether or not this building had originally been used as a shed, parts of it certainly were in the latter days of steam shunting power within the works. These duties started to be taken over by diesels in early 1965, although the W1 duty, (Works No 1), which tripped between the Works and the Basford Hall marshalling yards with material for the Works and the depot stores vans, etc, remained the preserve of an LMS Fowler '4F' until midsummer 1966. This was just about the last working of these engines, with Nos 44377 and 44525 allocated to the Works, and not recorded as withdrawn until October 1966.

Returning now to the 'small shed for banking engines' mentioned in the previous chapter, a GJR minute of 4 May 1842 records the need for a

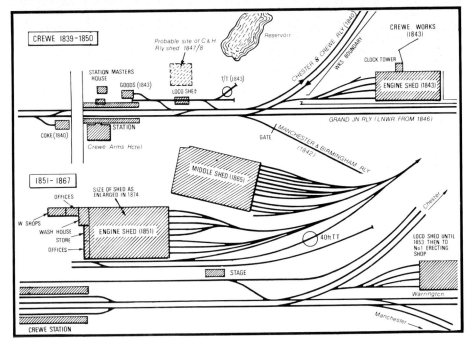

Above left:
**The Works No 1 Erecting Shop is seen here on the right, before 1930, and after being extended southwards — this was the 'engine in steam shed' referred to in this chapter; notice the clock tower to the centre. The shop originally terminated parallel with the tower, and the Signal Shop is to the left. The bridge on the right gave access over the main line to the Grease Works, and the church tower to the left is Christ Church, built by the railway and consecrated in 1845.** *Collection R. A. Griffiths*

'large turntable at Crewe to turn engines and tenders together', but nothing seems to have been done. On 8 June, Norris and Trevithick were requested to prepare a plan and estimate for a shed for 'engines in steam' at Crewe, and in October that year Norris was being asked to report on a site for a proposed temporary engine shed at Crewe. Francis Trevithick was of course Northern Division Locomotive Superintendent of the LNWR until 1853, and he had been resident engineer during the construcion of the GJR under Joseph Locke. He had taken charge of the workshops at Edge Hill as Locomotive Superintendent in 1841, and was responsible for much of the layout and equipment of Crewe Works. It should be recalled that on formation of the LNWR three Divisions were created: Northern, Southern and North Eastern, the Southern broadly corresponding to the London & Birmingham Railway, with its locomotive headquarters at Wolverton, the Northern combining the activities of the other former companies except the Manchester & Birmingham, with headquarters at Crewe, and the much smaller North Eastern Division, with headquarters at Longsight, Manchester, looking after the Manchester & Birmingham. In August 1857 the Northern and North Eastern Divisions combined, Trevithick — an extremely controversial character by all accounts — retired, and the erstwhile North Eastern Superintendent John Ramsbottom took over. During all this time the redoubtable John McConnell presided over activities at Wolverton, but in March 1862 the Northern and Southern Divisions were also amalgamated under Ramsbottom, with headquarters somewhat naturally at Crewe. In the following year he introduced a number code for the railway's locomotive sheds and Crewe took the number 15, which it retained until the LMS introduced its new system in 1935.

Richard Stuart Norris had also been employed by Locke from the early days of the GJR construction, and as resident engineer of the Northern Division of the LNWR, he was responsible for much of the early developments of not only Crewe Works, but also the town of Crewe itself. After a spell as Northern Superintendent and Engineer, he retired in 1862.

Following the 1847 directors' request, no trace of the findings can be located but, in February 1848,

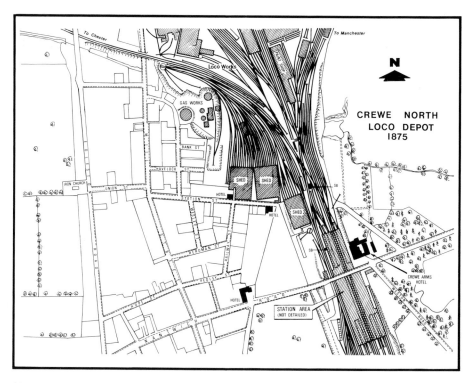

Above:
**Crewe North in 1875, from the First Edition 25in Ordnance Survey map, Notice Nos 1, 2 and 3 Sheds, before construction of the Stock Shed and station enlargements.**

Trevithick was pointing out to the directors that the forthcoming opening of the line to Chester would require more engine shed space at Crewe. On 4 April that year, Norris presented tenders for the temporary shed, although nowhere does it become obvious why a permanent building could not be erected. The tenders varied between £1,603 and £1,883 and, predictably, the cheapest was selected. Unlike the 1847 scheme, this shed does seem to have been built, because a minute dated 19 September 1848 recorded 'that the temporary engine shed on the westward side of the line at Crewe was blown down recently by a hurricane'. It was resolved that it be rebuilt, 'upon an improved construction'.

During 1850 Trevithick reported that of the 262 engines employed on the Northern Division, there was only shed accommodation for 178; he therefore recommended erection of a new shed for 20 engines at Crewe. Norris submitted plans for such a shed on 22 April that year at a cost of £2,500, but nothing seems to have been done pending these two worthies visiting the new Great Northern Railway (GNR) shed at King's Cross in London — presumably reckoned to be a model of its kind. On 17 June 1851, and one can only presume that

it was following this visit, Norris submitted revised plans for a shed to hold 16 engines, and estimated to cost £3,000.

One is left wondering what happened to the engines in the period since the temporary shed was blown down, but perhaps the No 1 Erecting Shop was still in use as an engine shed of sorts, or at least a part of it. In 1853 Trevithick reported that 'the old engine in steam shed has been converted into a workshop' — this statement giving credence to the theory already outlined. In 1857 some 64 persons were recorded as being employed in the 'steam sheds' at Crewe.

The next mention of locomotive sheds at Crewe in the directors' minutes comes in 1858, when plans and estimates were required for the enlargement of the shed; so the 1851 plans seem, on this occasion at least, to have been actioned. It would seem that by about 1859, an eight-road brick-built shed existed, just north of the station platforms, west of the line, and generally in the area later used in the 1896-1904 Crewe remodelling, which included the new independent goods lines. This shed was 235ft long and 145ft wide, with four hipped roofs each covering two roads, and a 40ft diameter turntable was erected north of it, together with offices and workshops to the south. A coaling shed with water tank above, of typical LNWR style, was situated between this shed and the main lines, and the coal road for the engines was between the stage and the shed itself.

In 1863, estimates were once again being sought for shed enlargements, and they resulted in proposals for a completely new 12-road shed, west of the existing one, at a cost of £8,303. The proposals were accepted, and the new shed, which logically became the No 2 Shed, opened in 1865. This building, the famous Middle Shed of later years, existed until the depot closed in 1965, and became the centre of mechanical activity and nucleus of the entire depot. Measuring 230ft × 170ft the shed's 12 roads were divided equally under three hipped roofs, and it became one of the first of a series of standard LNWR sheds built to this pattern, albeit of differing configurations. The style was later superseded by the

Webb Northlight pattern, and events were to dictate that these later types had roof structures that were not nearly as long-lasting. This No 2 Shed at Crewe, together with another still to be described at Willesden, are examples of the earlier design that lasted well into the 1960s.

The new shed at Crewe was eventually well-equipped, with a wheeldrop, shear lifting legs and an extensive workshop with a variety of machine tools. Hence my earlier reference to it becoming the centre of mechanical activity, as opposed to servicing and stabling of loco-motives.

Continued expansion of traffic and, therefore, locomotive allocation at Crewe, soon necessitated yet another

Above:
**Two views of Crewe North Shed taken on 3 April 1913. The top view shows very clearly the six hipped-roofed sections of the Middle and Abba Sheds, and beyond them the northlight roof of the Stock Shed; note the fine array of LNWR motive power. The wagons in the foreground all carried locomotive coal from the North Staffordshire coalfields, from where the bulk of Crewe's locomotive coal came. The lower view shows the Stock Shed and yard, with the skip hoist for the coaling plant to the extreme right. The 'Claughton' class 4-6-0 in the centre is No 2222 *Sir Gilbert Claughton*, itself the prototype of the class, and the only one delivered by this date — hence the certainty of its identification. Notice the 'Experiment' class 4-6-0 to the left with its centre pair of wheels removed, no doubt due to a hot box.** *Collection A. G. Ellis*

shed, and an October 1866 list gives Crewe a total allocation of 150 locomotives. Therefore in 1867 construction of a further 12-road shed commenced. Completed in 1868, this, the No 3 Shed known more popularly as the 'Abyssinia', or just 'Abba' (for details of the origin of this name see chapter 4) — came into use in July. Although basically the same size and design as the Middle Shed, the four westernmost roads were shorter than the remainder, at 145ft long each, and this reduced capacity by around one locomotive in each of these roads. This shorter section, always known as the Cage (for reasons I have been unable to discover) was necessary to allow the continued existence of the Queens Hotel, at the extreme end of a row of terraced cottages in Station Street. The alternative would have been to move the whole building northwards but, as it would not then have had its front end in line with the Middle Shed, problems would have been encountered in the layout of the yard, hence the need for this shorter section.

The Queens Hotel was a hallowed establishment in the eyes of many of the sheds' human occupants, and indeed remained so until final closure of the depot. Along with the whole of Station Street itself, and much of the

surrounding property, it was demolished very soon afterwards. Another event in 1868 was the diversion of the Chester line as it left Crewe, a new route known as the Deviation line coming into use on 26 July. This line took a course south of the original one, and allowed expansion of the Old Works and construction of the new and aptly named Deviation Works. It rejoined the original route about a mile further on. It had the effect, however, of reducing the area of the shed yard somewhat.

After the completion of Abba, the shed servicing facilities were taken in hand for improvement, and a new 45ft diameter turntable was installed towards the north end of the yard, and almost behind the enginemen's barracks in Mill Street. Additionally, a large 110ft × 30ft double-sided brick built coaling shed was erected, and locomotives could be coaled either side simultaneously, with the coal wagons standing on the two parallel internal roads. About the same time, and to give additional yard space, the No 1 Shed turntable was moved, and resited south of the shed building. By 1878 the number of drivers, firemen and cleaners employed in the sheds at Crewe had risen to no less than 560, and the locomotive allocation numbered 140.

Above:
'Patriot' No 45503 *The Royal Leicestershire Regiment*, seen here on 20 August 1955 at her home depot, and standing on one of the roads built to radiate around the 1950-built 70ft turntable. This was before construction of the lightweight semi-roundhouse. Notice on the left the remains of the roof of Abba, and the building immediately to the right of this, which is the rear of the Queens Hotel. Further right can be seen the rear of the terraced houses in Station Street, and in the extreme left-hand corner what had been No 5 road in Abba, by this time roofless. *Brian Morrison*

To enable the station to be extended in the period 1875-79, which included the construction of the island platform that was numbered 3 and 4 from 1913 to 1984 (and is currently platform faces 6 and 11), it was necessary to demolish part of the No 1 Shed. The demolition removed one of the hip-roofed sections completely, that nearest the station, and thus the two westernmost roads disappeared, a new outer wall being constructed. To compensate for this loss of two roads, at the same time the shed was extended northwards until its western wall abutted the No 2 — Middle Shed due to the angle between the two, making its total length around 300ft and its width 100ft. At the same time the coaling stage had to be dismantled, and the whole of the activities west of the new shed wall were swept away to allow for the station enlargements. By this time, of course, the shed's coaling and locomotive servicing facilities had been considerably augmented by the new facilities built in connection with the erection of the Middle and Abba Sheds.

Crewe North became the site of one of the earliest attempts to mechanise the disagreeable task of coaling steam locomotives when, some time in the early 1890s, a 100ft × 60ft coaling shed was built, in front of Abba Shed, and locomotives were coaled by a system of hydraulic bucket cranes. Although not completely mechanised, this arrangement greatly reduced the manual labour involved, and became a very identifiable feature of photographs taken at Crewe North until it was demolished after erection of a new plant commissioned in 1909.

Some time in the early 1890s (unfortunately it has not been possible to track down a more precise date, but probably late 1891 or early 1892) a further 12-road shed was built west of Abba, this time of the Webb Northlight pattern and measuring 255ft long and 155ft wide. The front of this shed was not quite in line with Abba, but its rear wall was parallel with the shortened section of that shed — the section known as the Cage. The construction of this shed necessitated the demolition of what was left of the original Crewe Gas Works, situated in Lockett Street and dating from 1842-43. This had been railway-owned and built, initially to

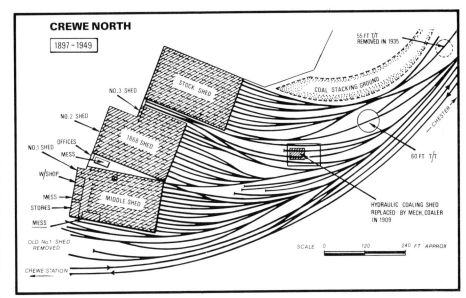

supply the workshops and other railway activities, but from 1850-51 had been extended to provide a town supply. After commissioning of the Steel Works in 1864, the consumption of gas increased to such an extent that a new gas works was necessary, and erection of this plant commenced in Wistaston Road. Large extensions to that works in the period 1882-86 saw the final demise of the Lockett Street establishment.

Between Abba and the new shed there were two uncovered roads, one of which was used by locomotives going to and from the new hydraulic coaling plant, and the other for coal wagons waiting to be used at the coal stage; there was a system of capstans to haul the wagons to the stage, and save locomotive power. This coal stage was situated in the yard between the respective fans of roads serving this new shed and Abba, and

when replaced the new plant was in the same place, and served by the same means. This area between the two sheds was known as the 'Ghost of Abyssinia', and there was an arrangement to spray the coal in the wagons so as to lay the dust; unsuspecting new entrants were sent to discover the 'Ghost', only to have a water spray turned on to them!

Always known as the Stock Shed, the new building seems to have been used for most of its life to house

Below:
**This photograph of Pacific No 6229 *Duchess of Hamilton* would appear to date from late 1938, when the locomotive was new, in streamlined form and maroon livery. It is standing outside Abba, with the Stock Shed in the background; notice how the locomotive contrasts sharply against the gloomy surroundings of the shed yard.** *Ian Allan Library*

locomotives either waiting attention in the Works, or recently outshopped and waiting their first allocations — hence its name. Standard LNWR practice was to allocate locomotives which had received attention in the Works to the first shed that needed a locomotive of that type rather than to return locomotives to the shed from whence they had come. Hence a shed sending in, say, a 'Prince of Wales' 4-6-0 for overhaul, would be allocated either one recently outshopped, or the next one to become available after overhaul. The Stock Shed was used to store locomotives in these circumstances. This practice was claimed to improve locomotive availability, in that sheds always had their full allocation quota, and the pool of spare engines was smaller than if each shed had to cover its own requirements when locomotives were away for Works overhaul. It is also the reason why LNWR locomotive allocations rarely remained static.

During World War 2 many of the American S160 2-8-0 engines imported into this country and awaiting shipment to the Continent were stored in this shed. Also, many of the British-built 'Austerity' 2-8-0s and 2-10-0s that had put in some service on British railways and were later shipped overseas had their motions stripped and other work carried out on them in the Stock Shed prior to shipment. After the war a lot of machinery was stored in this shed, in particular machine tools ordered by the Ministry of Supply for the war effort but no longer needed after cessation of hostilities.

Following the completion of the Stock Shed, and for a short period of around four or five years, Crewe North presented a vista of no less than 42 covered roads. This was by far and away larger than any other establishment in this country, either before or since.

In the latter part of the 19th century it became increasingly apparent that Crewe was becoming an enormous bottleneck, with its junctions bringing no less than seven separate traffic flows together, if one includes traffic to Liverpool; the marshalling yards south of the station were bursting. To combat this a very bold plan was hatched, the first surveys for which in 1894 indicated that no less than 1,000 trains per day were passing through Crewe. There were three paramount needs: first, to enlarge the marshalling yards; secondly, to enlarge the

passenger station, and thirdly, as far as possible to keep the goods and mineral movements away from the passenger trains. The developed scheme entailed building Independent goods lines, burrowing in tunnels in places, which — together with station enlargements — resulted in the need for additional space west of the existing station. To provide this the remainder of the No 1 Shed had to be demolished. The demolition seems to have taken place around 1898; certainly a new shed to replace it, south of the station and adjacent to the revised marshalling yards, opened on 1 October 1897. This was Crewe South shed.

We have already seen how the 1879 station improvements caused the erection of a new island platform, west of the original one, and the 1896-1904 improvements involved construction of another island, west of the other two. The combined effect of these two sets of improvements was to increase the station area from 93 acres to no less than 223 acres. Currently not in use for passenger traffic, this island provided the main platforms for northbound traffic, with its outer faces numbered 1 and 2 until the recent remodelling. During the 1988 summer season it is intended to bring into use again the former Platform 2.

Naturally, when the No 1 Shed was demolished, with it went what was left of its servicing facilities, and the turntable. However, about the same time — 1897 — the newer 45ft turntable, north of the main sheds,

was replaced by one of 55ft diameter, situated more towards the centre of the shed yard. This was converted to electric drive in 1920, one of few such turntables in this country, although the Lancashire & Yorkshire Railway (LYR) had a number.

Towards the end of the remodelling works in 1904, the shed facilities were again increased and the Middle Shed was extended southwards by 40ft, encompassing part of Station Street, and allowing considerable increase in the space between the end of the roads and the new back wall of the shed. This was to provide room for additional workshop space, offices, mess rooms and a large stores building to the southwest corner of the shed. On the debit side, these works caused the demolition of the North Western Hotel, which was situated on the opposite side of Station Street to the Queens Hotel. Also in the space south of the shed, a large new office block was erected, to provide not only for the shed's administration, but also as headquarters office for the Crewe District. Presumably the acquisition of a part of Station Street, which had hitherto extended to abut the main line, entailed a compulsory purchase order. About the same time that these works were underway, workshops

Below:
**Crewe North in 1910, from the Third Edition 25in Ordnance Survey map. Changes since 1875 include the demolition of No 1 Shed and the construction of the Stock Shed and the Independent lines.**

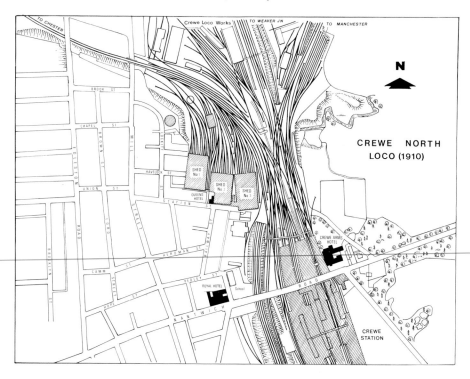

were erected for the Outdoor Machinery Department and these, along with the shed offices, remained until the final closure of the shed in 1965. Also in this area was the filter plant, where water from the company's reservoirs at Whitmore and Madeley, both south of Crewe and alongside the main line, was filtered before use. As with gas, the railway company provided the town with most of its water.

The demolition of the No 1 Shed and the building of the Stock Shed saw the completion of the covered facilities at Crewe North so far as the LNWR was concerned. Of course, the depot only assumed the suffix 'North' after completion of the new shed south of the station, which naturally became Crewe South, in 1897. Suffixes were added to Crewe Shed's number code, the South Shed becoming 15S and Whitchurch 15W.

There were now three 12-road sheds: there were two in the Ramsbottom period hipped-roofed pattern — the new No 1 (always known as Middle) and the new No 2 (always known as Abba) — and the New No 3, the Webb Northlight-pattern shed, the Stock Shed, which never seems to have been referred to by its natural number. In 1913 a total of 700 men were employed at the North and South Sheds.

One further development needs to be chronicled under the LNWR years. In 1909 the first completely mechanised locomotive coaling plant in the country was commissioned. This all-steel erection became an extremely prominent landmark in Crewe, and had a bunker capacity of 270 tons, differing from later plants in its use of a skip hoist to elevate the coal into the bunker, rather than elevating the whole railway wagon. The loaded railway wagons were first of all placed into a circular tippler, which turned them around and discharged their contents into an underground bunker; from there the coal was fed into the skips, which were hoisted up to the main bunker, ready for discharge into locomotive tenders. The plant was designed and built jointly by the LNWR and Babcock & Wilcox, and although apparently successful, does not seem to have been perpetuated to any great extent anywhere else. It could deal with no less than four locomotives simultaneously, being built on the site of the earlier hydraulic coal stage, parts of which remained in existence for many years; just how locomotives were coaled during the construction has gone unrecorded. The remains of the wagon tippler were still in existence when the depot closed in 1965.

Above:
**The North Shed Barracks, derelict by the time this photograph was taken in June 1973, with Mill Street in the foreground and the Chester line passing over the bridge behind. The North Shed itself was to the right, and the Old Works to the rear. Presumably, the bay window to the right of the building, was part of the House Superintendent's quarters!** *Allan Baker*

Before concluding the history of Crewe North in the LNWR period, it should be mentioned that in 1867 the railway company had built an 'Enginemen's Barracks', containing 42 beds, on the site of some old flour mills in Mill Street — hence the street's name. This was for drivers and firemen from other depots who had to spend time at Crewe between turns, and the building was immediately on the south side of the bridge carrying the Chester line over Mill Street, and on the east side of the roadway. Latterly derelict, it lasted until about 1970. A second and much more modern barracks, situated in Gresty Road, opened coincident with the South Shed in 1897. During World War 2, this barracks was extended to the rear, when guards working away from their home depots were also allowed to use it, and there was a general increase in lodging owing to the vagaries of the timetable in wartime. By December 1925 the

North barracks was recorded as having 67 beds, and the south 66 beds, and as there were no obvious signs of extensions at the north, one can only presume that the amount of space per man had been reduced! On closure shortly after World War 2, the North barracks became a Ministry of Labour hostel. At this date the North Shed employed 1,404 footplatemen and had an allocation of 147 engines; the South Shed then employed 254 men and had 144 engines. Clearly, many North Shed men must have worked on South Shed-allocated power. The Locomotive Foreman's salary was but £575. Whitchurch, a sub-shed of Crewe North, found employment for 23 men and seven engines at this date. This sub-shed of Crewe North housed the locomotives that worked the branch from Whitchurch to Chester via Broxton, as well as providing locomotives for trains off the Cambrian system. The Cambrian Railways also had some men stationed at Whitchurch, and an agreement with the LNWR to use the shed facilities.

There were few developments to the facilities at Crewe North during the interwar years, except for the general concentration of the heavier repairs and maintenance there, resulting from the LMS Motive Power Area Locomotive Supply, Repair, Concentration & Garage Scheme of 1932. The theory here was that by concentrating all repairs and main-tenance on locomotives allocated to a Motive Power Area at one shed, economies in facilities, manpower and locomotives would accrue. Thus, each Motive Power Area had one depot, enhanced as necessary, in terms of manpower and facilities, encompassing all the maintenance — except the X day examinations and running repairs — to the entire fleet of locomotives allocated to the area, the other depots being known as 'Garages'.

By having sufficient 'Maintenance Spare' locomotives at the one depot, and feeding them to the garages as necessary to cover other locomotives at the concentration depot for atten-tion, theory had it that less in total were needed. Of course, particular locomotives did not become per-manent spares, but any one available at the time was used. Likewise, by concentrating manpower and facili-ties, machine tools, etc, at one depot, less were needed. The scheme, the brainchild of Lemon, Urie and Rudgard, was pursued with much vigour, along with the associated Locomotive Maintenance & Mechanical Efficiency Scheme, or X scheme as it became known: it was very much a case of woe betide any transgressing Shed-master . . . !

E. J. H. Lemon was Operating Vice-President of the LMS, and had been Chief Mechanical Engineer (CME) in the interregnum of 1931, between the retirement of Sir Henry Fowler and the appointment of W. A. Stanier. He was very much an organiser, and had previously been in charge of the Carriage & Wagon Department which henceforth came under the combined control of the CME. Ernest Lemon trained with the North British Locomotive Co in Glasgow and joined the Midland Railway in 1917, having previously spent some time with the Highland Railway. On Stanier's appointment he went on to become Vice President of the LMS, with special responsibility for all operating aspects, hence his keen interest in improving locomotive availability and efficiency. It must be remembered at this juncture that the LMS had adopted the Midland Railway practice whereby the locomotive running department did not come under the control of the Chief Mechanical Engineer, but under a separate chief. This practice had not been followed by any of the other LMS constituents in pre-grouping days.

Below:
**A view taken in 1936 of the North Shed, from the coaling plant, and showing on the right the three hip-roofed sections of the Middle Shed. In the background can be seen the 'Spider Bridge', which connected the Works with the station. By this date few of the old LNWR types remained, and only a 'Prince of Wales' 4-6-0 and a 'Box Tank' can be discerned amid the many Stanier and Fowler types.** *Collection Harry Newbiggin*

Lemon was assisted by D. C. Urie — son of R. W. Urie, one time CME of the LSWR — who became Superintendent of Motive Power at the same time, having previously been Mechanical Engineer in charge of matters north of the border; prior to this he had been the last CME of the Highland Railway, albeit for a very short period. Last, but as events were to prove by no means least, was the redoubtable Lt-Col Harold Rudgard — another extremely strong personality, ex-Midland Railway and imbued with all that meant — who assisted Urie and eventually took over the reins from him in 1943. On Nationalisation, Rudgard became Motive Power Chief for the entire British Railways: needless to say, thereafter former LMS practices and procedures in the operation of locomotives and their depots were promulgated with the utmost despatch over the whole system.

Under the X scheme arrangements locomotives were 'stopped' at preset intervals, depending on the work they did and the periodicity between boiler washouts; the latter largely depending on the quality of feed water in the areas the locomotives worked. On the X day preventative maintenance and examinations would be carried out, with the intention that the locomotive would then run to its next X day exam without needing any attention, other than minor running repairs and servicing, and certainly without the need to drop the fire. Of course, there were always exceptions, but by and large it worked, and showed marked improvements in reliability and availability. The remainder of the maintenance was divided into those parts which moved — like valves, pistons and valve gear parts — and which were examined on a mileage basis, and those components which did not move — like boiler fittings — which were examined on a strict periodicity basis. Thus, a locomotive could be 'stopped' for an X exam (Class 7, 6 and 5XP passenger engines, 6-8 days; passenger and freight tender engines, 12-16 days; other types, 24-32 days), with or without a boiler washout, and the Crewe locomotives generally managed two weeks between such attention (BFX = Boiler Full X; WOX = Washout X). Alternatively a locomotive could be 'stopped' for an X exam combined with say, a 3-5 or 7-9 week periodic exam and, if due, a mileage exam too. The latter were undertaken at 5,000-6,000-mile intervals, the No 1 examination occurring at that mileage, and the No 8 exam at 40,000-48,000 miles. Prior to the introduction of this scheme it was possible and not unusual for a locomotive to be 'stopped' on three or more separate occasions within a few weeks, and for different items of maintenance and repair to be undertaken, not counting the boiler washout. In essence the X scheme undertook an element of preventative maintenance when the locomotive was 'stopped' for its routine washout, and carried out any other due maintenance at the same time: it effected any repairs that were necessary — or which might become critical before the next X day — so as to ensure (as far as possible) that the locomotive would run with the minimum of attention until it had to be 'stopped' again for another washout. This system remained in use for the life of the steam locomotive in BR service, and a derivative of it was developed — and is still in use — for the newer forms of traction that replaced steam.

The Crewe Motive Power Area, under the charge of a District Motive Power Superintendent, consisted of Crewe North (coded 5A under the 1935 scheme), Crewe South (5B), Whitchurch (a sub shed of Crewe North and not coded), Stafford (5C, a sub-shed of Crewe North), Alsager (5F, a sub-shed of Crewe South), Stoke (5D), and Uttoxeter (5E, a sub-shed of Stoke). Despite much new equipment, in particular new machine tools being provided at Crewe North, the independent NSR lived on and, apart from wheeldrop work, very few locomotives headed north from the Potteries towards Cheshire for repairs, Col Rudgard or no Col Rudgard! Prior to the closure of Stoke Workshops on 31 December 1926, the NSR section locomotives had continued to be repaired there, and as this was alongside the running shed, the latter had no facilities for removing locomotive wheels, although very well equipped in all other spheres; thus, NSR-section locomotives had to come to Crewe for this type of work after the workshops closed.

The only other improvements that seem to have been made by the LMS at Crewe North were, first, the replacement of the 55ft turntable with a new vacuum-operated one of 60ft diameter located south of the existing table, and enabling the then new 'Royal Scot' 4-6-0s to be turned. The old table was left in situ until around 1935, and its filled-in pit could still be located until the depot closed. This turntable was very soon outmoded however, and with the introduction of the Pacifics in 1933, which needed a 70ft table, problems arose. Secondly, some mechanisation of the ash handling arrangements took place, and an ash elevator was constructed so that ashes could be discharged into rail wagons without manual effort. All heavy repairs and maintenance were concentrated in the Middle Shed, with Abba becoming very much a running shed.

Before progressing the history of the shed any further, mention needs to be made of the breakdown arrangements. The Locomotive Department of the LNWR, as on all other railways, assumed responsibility for clearance of the line after derailments, collisions or other mishaps. Like all other companies the LNWR soon equipped itself with special trains to carry tools and other gear, so as to be able to attend such incidents, and usually converted old rolling stock for this purpose. These facilities were generally followed by the acquisition of railborne hand cranes, and such equipment existed at Crewe from an early date.

However, unlike its contemporaries, the LNWR was slow to adopt steam cranes and it would seem that the invincible and authoritative Francis William Webb, Chief Mechanical Engineer from 1871 to 1903, did not approve of such things. He preferred, no doubt much to the chagrin of the civil engineers, to haul errant locomotives back on to the rails by means of ramps, packing and as many hauling locomotives as were needed! But problems were encountered, and following a spate of quite major incidents (like the Preston derailment of 1896), when the clearing up operations were quite obviously severely hampered by the lack of a modern steam crane, questions were asked. Indeed, by this time the technology of such cranes was becoming quite sophisticated, and they were being designed for loads up to 20 tons. There were occasions when the mighty LNWR was reduced to borrowing steam cranes, and did so on 8 December 1899 when the 'Irish Mail' came to grief at Norton Bridge, just north of Stafford. On this occasion, and indeed on several others around that time, the NSR Cowans Sheldon 15-ton crane (No 1965 of 1895) came to the rescue.

In later years when Crewe did get a crane, it was often to be seen on 'twin' lifts with this NSR machine, on both scheduled bridge lifting jobs and derailments, and on the systems of both companies. This practice continued after grouping. On 11 June 1897 there occurred a nasty derailment at Welshampton on the Cambrian Railways, and the Crewe breakdown gang went along to assist their Welsh colleagues. At that time even the apparently penniless Cambrian aspired to a modern 15-ton crane, albeit a hand-operated one. The story goes that during a double lift, whilst the Cambrian fellows lifted their end with commensurate ease, Crewe's archaic 10-ton hand crane would not move its end by as much as an inch! When Mr Webb heard about these proceedings, and his company's disgrace, he was far from amused; orders went out forthwith for a steam crane! But as this was to be a steam crane to beat all other steam cranes (as was Webb's bent), nothing from any of the established crane manufacturers would satisfy

him, and a crane would therefore be designed and built at Crewe! This decision seems to have been a mistake, because the final result, despite being no less than eight years in the making, was by all accounts little short of a disaster.

Construction of this four-wheeled vertical-boilered 20-ton crane seems to have commenced in 1897, but it was not completed until long after Webb's retirement, indeed not until 1905. Doubtless he soon forgot the Welshampton incident, and his staff at Crewe the crane! In any event, it must have been built at an extremely sedentary pace, and largely by trial and error. George Whale, on appointment to succeed Webb, seems to have quickened the pace somewhat — perhaps he was fed up with seeing the bits laying around the shops — and on completion the crane was allocated to the Crewe North breakdown train. Little about its use seems to have been recorded, and perhaps this is indicative of its unpopularity: the crane appears to have been judged by anyone who ever had

anything to do with it as one of Crewe's few failures. In any event it did not take George Whale long to order purpose-built cranes from established builders, and the first arrived at Rugby from Cowans Sheldon of Carlisle in 1909 — a 25-ton crane — and in the following year Crewe got a splendid Ransomes & Rapier 36-ton crane, Ransomes works number B5049.

The Crewe product was foisted on the unsuspecting Willesden and, after an accident inolving the lifting of a 4-4-0 tender engine somewhere in the London area — or so the tale goes — in 1915 it migrated to Crewe Works for repairs and modifications, but in effect was laid aside, unsung and certainly unwanted! The intervention of World War 1 gave the opportunity not only for this crane to live another

Below:
**Drawing dated November 1936 showing the southern end of the Middle Shed before construction of the canteen and offices. This plan was connected with proposed improvements, not all of which actually materialised.**

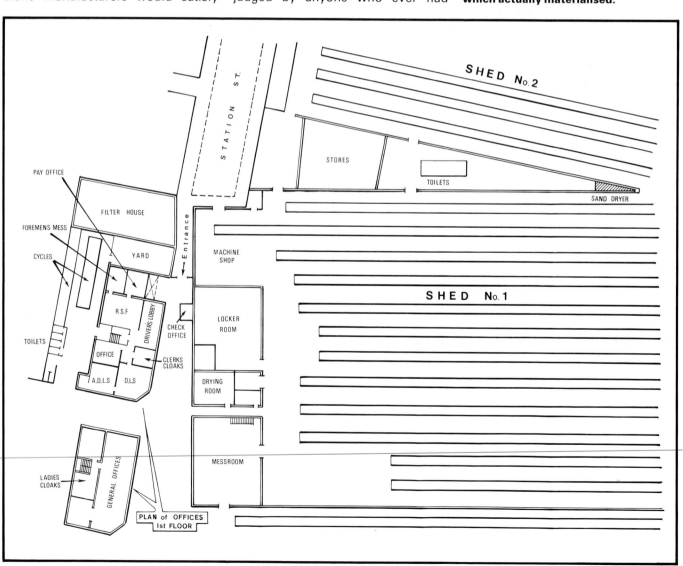

day, but also for the LNWR to be rid of it to the War Department, by the latter's helpful requisition! Doubtless everybody at Crewe (and of course Willesden) heaved a sigh of relief, but the opinions of those who had to work it in the future have gone unrecorded. . . . Indeed, nothing further is known about Crewe's only entry into the steam breakdown crane business, except that the crane was shipped for use somewhere overseas. Once rid of it, the LNWR wasted no time in ordering a replacement for Willesden, doubtless with the money from the War Department, and a brand new Cowans Sheldon 36-ton crane arrived there in 1917. The Crewe Ransomes crane was soon joined by two of the four former 34ft six-wheel radial-axle sleeping cars of 1881 vintage (originally built for the 'Irish Mail') to be used as riding vans for the crew. Numbered 2149A and

2150A, they had been rebuilt as bogie vehicles and renumbered into the duplicate list with the 'A' prefix, in 1910. There was also a specially built 40ft bogie van for tools and equipment, and this ensemble, one of the smartest breakdown turn-outs on the LNWR if not in the country, remained as the Crewe North equipment for many years.

At grouping the Ransomes crane became No MP 7 (ie Motive Power Department Crane No 7) in a combined LMS list, and remained at Crewe North until transfer in 1939 to Newton Heath; it came back to Crewe for use in the Works yard in 1954, and ended its days there — renumbered RS1012 — in 1966. It was replaced by a 1930-built Cowans Sheldon 36-ton crane (No MP 4), which had been at

Above:
**One of the tool vans, an interesting old vehicle, built at Wolverhampton in 1902 as West Coast Joint Stock 50ft Corridor Brake Third No 75; (to Diagram D 67) becoming LMS No 6759 (later 6049). It passed into Departmental stock in November 1942, initially as a Tool Van at the South Shed.**
*Collection Harry Newbiggin*

Leeds Holbeck since new, but had then just been returned from its makers where it had been uprated to 50 tons capacity. This crane, later renumbered RS 1005/50 — ie Railway/Steam No 1005 with a 50-ton capacity — was a splendid piece of equipment, and remained at Crewe for the remainder of its life, going to the South Shed on closure of the North in 1965, and on to the Diesel

Right:
**An aerial view of the North Shed taken about 1947, and showing, left to right, the Stock Shed — largely roofless and with some tracks apparently missing — Abba, with smoke vents indicating its use for engines in steam, and to the right the Middle Shed. The roof of this last shed was without smoke vents by this date, indicating its use for locomotives under repair. The higher roof section, over part of the left-hand hip roof, was to accommodate the shear lifting legs and wheel drop. The shorter section of Abba, known as the Cage, can be seen, as can the Queens Hotel. This was before any work started on the modernisation scheme, and the mechanical coaling plant can be seen, along with the Old Works No 1 erecting shop, one time 'engine in steam shed', to the top left centre.**
*Collection R. A. Griffiths*

Depot when the South Shed closed in 1967; it was itself withdrawn from service in 1981.

Obviously the shed and its engines were worked extremely hard during World War 2, and with a minimum of maintenance. On cessation of hostilities all the buildings were badly in need of attention; the Stock Shed was largely roofless, and used for the storage of locomotives and miscellaneous departmental vehicles. Abba was used as the main running shed, and because of this its roof was in poor shape, whilst all the repair work was concentrated in the Middle Shed, including most of the X scheme examinations. The roof of this shed, although far from perfect, was in the best condition of all.

A long-overdue scheme was therefore put in hand early in 1948 (originally drawn up by the LMS) to completely renew the facilities at Crewe North, together with the construction of a completely new shed for the 'concentration' repairs, to be built south of the station and, in effect

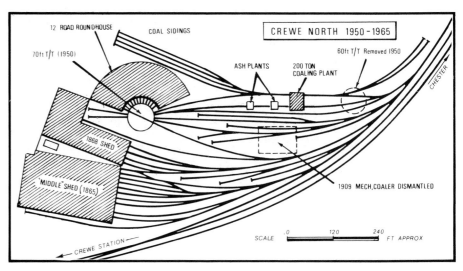

CREWE NORTH 1950-1965

12 ROAD ROUNDHOUSE — COAL SIDINGS
70ft T/T (1950)
ASH PLANTS — 200 TON COALING PLANT
60ft T/T Removed 1950
CHESTER
1868 SHED
'MIDDLE' SHED (1865)
1909 MECH.COALER DISMANTLED
CREWE STATION
SCALE .0 — 120 — 240 FT APPROX

almost midway between North and South Sheds — see Chapter 7. Thus, Crewe North would become a 'garage' itself — in LMS parlance — acting as a running depot and undertaking locomotive servicing, X examinations, washouts and the smaller repairs. All the large work, generally that where engines would not be steam, would go to the new

Below:
**A nice atmospheric pictue showing Rebuilt 'Scot' No 46106 *Gordon Highlander* sporting a 5A shed plate, and standing outside No 7 road of the Middle Shed on 20 August 1955. This locomotive was unique among its sisters, having BR Standard type smoke deflectors. With a train reporting number on the smokebox headboard, presumably she is about to take up a special working.** *Brian Morrison*

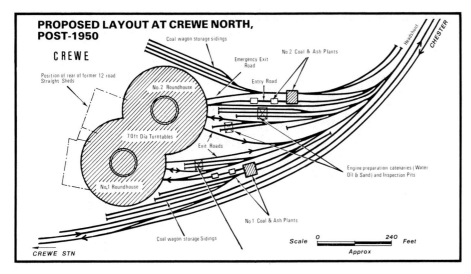

Coal wagon storage sidings
No 2 Coal & Ash Plants
Emergency Exit Road
Entry Road
Position of rear of former 12 road Straight Sheds
No. 2 Roundhouse
70ft Dia Turntables
Exit Roads
No.1 Roundhouse
Engine preparation catenaries (Water Oil & Sand) and Inspection Pits
No 1 Coal & Ash Plants
Coal wagon storage Sidings
CREWE STN
Healdshut
CHESTER
Scale 0 240 Feet
Approx

depot. Events dictated that much of these plans would be stillborn, and as will be seen in Chapter 7, the new depot was turned over to diesel traction even before it was finally completed. The North Shed meanwhile was left to soldier on until the end of steam, with limited improvements.

The original plan, which was estimated to cost around £1 million, excluding the new depot south of the station, envisaged the complete demolition of all the shed buildings on the site, and their replacement by two 280ft diameter 32-road roundhouses, of square construction. Each roundhouse would have a 70ft turntable, one building roughly occupying the site of the Stock Shed and part of Abba, and the other the Middle Shed and the remaining half of Abba. The roundhouses would have overlapped each other slightly, and have been interconnected, both structurally and by a common road. Each roundhouse would have been served by its own independent inlet roads, ash pits, coal and ash handling plants, preparation pits and outlet roads etc; indeed the two buildings were seen as two separate operations, both having all that was necessary to service and prepare steam locomotives for traffic. Thus, the throughput of locomotives would be increased and as a result the speed with which locomotives could be turned round between trips would be increased. It was hoped to improve locomotive availability by these means. Additionally of course, any breakdown of one set of facilities would not stop the shed functioning.

In 1950 a start was made on the project and, after demolition of the Stock Shed or what was left of it, the western parts of Abba were also demolished, and the first of the 70ft

vacuum operated unbalanced turntables, intended as the centre-piece of the No 2 roundhouse, was installed. Eventually, 14 pitted roads were constructed radiating from this turntable, in the area to the west and formerly occupied by the Stock Shed, and southwards where Nos 6-12 roads in Abba had been. To relieve the shed of some of its workload,

especially mileage examinations on all locomotives other than the Class 8 Pacifics, a number of fitters were loaned to Longsight Depot in Manchester to undertake the work there; it was 1953 before they returned.

The new turntable came into use in 1950 and the roads radiating from it shortly afterwards. Subsequently, the old 60ft turntable was removed, as its site was needed for the new approach tracks to the coal and ash handling plants being built to serve the new

Below:
**The North Shed yard on 22 April 1950, showing Stanier Class 4 tank No 42454 and 'Compound' No 41117, standing respectively, outside Nos 11 and 10 roads of Abba Shed.**
*Collection R. A. Griffiths*

Bottom:
**Just eight days after the previous photograph was taken, the demolition of Abba begins. The part shown here is the shortened section known as The Cage, and the two roads to the right, between Abba and the Stock Shed, were known as 'The Ghost of Abyssinia'.** *Collection Harry Newbiggin*

**A nice array of motive power around the new 70ft turntable in 1957 and showing, left to right: 'Baby Scot' No 45544, '5XP' No 45592, another 'Baby Scot' No 45501, and then more '5XPs', Nos 45674, 45703 and 45586.**
*Martin Welch*

Below right:
**Another view of the roads built around the new turntable, this time showing 'Jubilee' No 45553 *Canada*, a long-serving Crewe North engine, on 15 March 1959. She is standing on one side of the roads later encompassed in the lightweight semi-roundhouse, and the pits are already constructed. Notice the water tank behind the engine, and the rear of the terraced houses in Station Street.** *K. R. Pirt*

this work was complete and construction of the new depot south of the station was underway, money seems to have dried up, and little further progress at Crewe North was made. Only the four easternmost roads of Abba retained their roof, and of this shed's other roads, only No 5 existed for its full length. However, the southern end of the shed roof, that over the various stores activities at the extreme ends of Nos 5-8 roads was left in situ, but the whole of the shorter section of this shed, the part known as the Cage, and covering Nos 9-12 roads, was demolished.

Matters then stagnated, apart from the completion of the new depot

south of the station, and then the Modernisation Plan announced the phasing out of steam in favour of diesel and electric traction. Nevertheless, conditions in the covered accommodation at Crewe North were becoming intolerable, and what was left of Abba's roof was so decayed as to be bordering on dangerous. A decision was, therefore, taken to build a lightweight semi-roundhouse over 12 of the roads that radiated from the new turntable, leaving the two nearest Abba uncovered. This structure was completed in 1959, and then gradually over the next few years, what remained of the roof over the four remaining roads in Abba was

roundhouse. These new facilities consisted of a reinforced concrete coaling plant with a bunker capacity of 200 tons capable of dealing with up to eight wagons an hour, each with a capacity of anywhere between eight and 21 tons. Coal was fed from the bunker to two independent roads, thereby allowing two locomotives to be fuelled simultaneously, via electrically operated vibrating feeders, which gave a continuous stream of coal at a rate of 2 tons/min. There were two mechanical ash plants with their associated tubs, also of reinforced concrete construction, and each with a bunker capacity of 25 tons of wet ash.

On completion of this work, which was known as stage one and came into use in mid-summer 1951, the old coal and ash plants, the former a landmark in Crewe for so many years, were largely dismantled. By the time

and were stabled there between turns.

Initially the diesel work was undertaken on No 2 road, but gradually as their numbers increased, the diesels encroached westwards, eventually occupying Nos 3, 4, 5 and 6 roads as well. During this period the steam breakdown crane always occupied No 1 road when not in use. In earlier days the breakdown vans had also been kept in the shed, on No 2 road, and before this had been stabled in the Stock Shed.

The fabric of the sheds continued to deteriorate, and the last remnants of Abba's roof came down in the winter of 1962-63, whilst the southern end of the Middle Shed became so leaky, that a temporary roof had to be erected underneath the existing one, consisting of corrugated asbestos sheeting supported by scaffolding poles. This covered the area at the southern (dead) ends of the roads, because this was the most populated area of the whole site, so far as human activity was concerned, and

this work took place during the early winter of 1963-64.

With the continued rundown of steam traction in the Crewe area, the need for two separate steam sheds grew less. Clearly the North Shed was better equipped than the South Shed, being the 'concentration' depot, but its condition was becoming very serious and roof falls were not uncommon, especially whenever there were high winds. A decision was therefore taken to modify the layout at the Diesel Depot, thus enabling it to undertake the daily diesel servicing commitment, and to spend the minimum amount of money on the facilities at Crewe South, so that that shed could undertake the heavier repairs and examinations to steam locomotives for the few years they had left. So, after 126 years the North Shed officially closed on and from 24 May 1965, exactly 100 years since the famous Middle Shed was first opened. I use the term 'officially', because this is not quite the end of the story. From that date the remaining steam locomotives allocated to the North Shed, consisting of but 38 locomotives, were transferred to Crewe South, and most of the maintenance and servicing staff dis-

Right:
**A friendly word from Inspector Bill Arnott, who might be suggesting that the driver should take it steady as he takes 'Royal Scot' No 46155** *The Lancer* **off the turntable at Crewe North in April 1964. The locomotive had just received attention on the wheeldrop, and by this time was bereft of its nameplates, and with little time to live. Beyond the engine are the former Abba Shed roads Nos 1-5, and beyond them the Middle Shed.** *E. N. Bellass*

Below:
**Pacific No 46254,** *City of Stoke-on-Trent*, **here standing in the North Shed yard in 1961, and after preparation for Royal train duties. Notice the burnished buffer faces, cylinder and valve chest covers, and the generally fine finish. Locomotives of this class, generally from the Crewe North allocation, continued on such duties over the West Coast route, well into diesel days. What a fine sight it presents.** *Neville Davies*

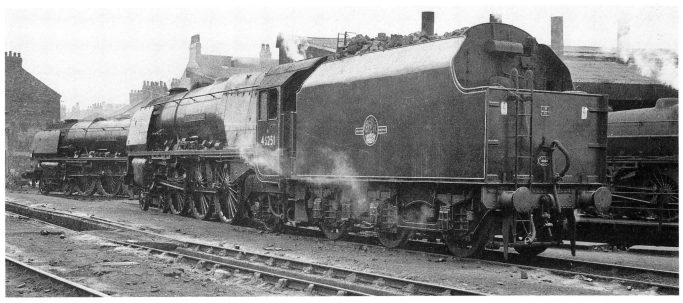

persed there, or to the Diesel Depot. The final allocation consisted of two Ivatt Class 2 2-6-2Ts, eight Class 5 4-6-0s, and 28 'Britannias'. Diesel locomotive servicing was tranferred to the Diesel Depot, with the new facilities there coming into use on the same date, and that depot then assumed the famous code 5A.

Footplate staff were moved to temporary accommodation in an otherwise redundant building known as the Bungalow, a single storey prefabricated building which was located on what remained of the mound of earth that had been excavated when the Independent line cuttings had been built. It was situated just north of the Diesel Depot, and almost alongside Platform 1 of the station, having originally been used as offices and a canteen. The longer-term plan for the footplatemen was to integrate them all, from both the North and South Sheds, but this had to wait several more years — see Chapter 3. However, the motive power management and much of the administration staff and activities were relocated in accommodation on the station at this

time. As facilities at Crewe South were not quite ready to take over the heavier steam repairs, a small number of staff remained at the North Shed to undertake this work, until they also departed for the South Shed when the residual work was transferred there on and from Monday 25 October 1965. The breakdown train had also remained at Crewe North during this period, as the staff who manned it at this time were largely those engaged on the heavier steam work.

Demolition was swift after complete closure; stop blocks were erected at the outer ends of a few of the Middle Shed roads as diesels continued to be stabled there between turns, following servicing at the Diesel Depot. The fuel storage tanks were eventually moved to the Diesel Depot to increase the storage capacity there, and the whole of the North Shed had been razed to the ground by early the following year; sections of it later became a car park. Since then parts of the site have been put to other uses, and the new power signalbox occupies part of it.

Above:
**A general view of the area between the Middle Shed and the roundhouse on 2 August 1963, showing the site of Abba.** *Martin Welch*

Above right:
**Another view of the same area, but looking towards the roundhouse and on the same day as the previous view. The building immediately behind the roundhouse is the Queens Hotel.** *Martin Welch*

Right:
**Three Pacifics on the site of Abba Shed, on 2 August 1963. From left to right; Nos 46237 *City of Bristol*, 46256 *Sir William A. Stanier FRS*, and 46228 *Duchess of Rutland*. The latter stands on what had been No 5 road in Abba Shed, and they are keeping company with Class 5 No 45142, and there is another Pacific behind. Notice roundhouse to left, the remains of the shed floor in the foreground, and the stored arch bricks.** *Martin Welch*

**Left:**
After closure and demolition of the North Shed, diesels continued to be stabled there between duties. The roads on which the locomotives illustrated are standing would have formerly continued into the Middle Shed. Crewe North Holding Sidings, as they were known, photographed in 1967, play host to, from left to right, Class 47s No D1947 (later 47504 and then 47702), D1720 (later 47129 and then 47658) with an unidentified Class 40 — all are in green livery. *R. G. Cooley*

**Below left:**
Photograph taken during the 1985 diversions, when the station was closed for extensive remodelling, looking north on 15 June; seen here is Class 85 No 85026 leaving the tunnel with an up train from the Liverpool line. Notice on the right the reinforced concrete footbridge, which was originally built to provide pedestrian access to Crewe North Shed, the site of which is just off the picture to the left. In the background the remodelling works can be seen well underway. *L. A. Nixon*

**Above right:**
Rail House provides a fine vantage point to view Crewe's railway activities. This view, looking north and taken on 27 February 1988, shows the Liverpool and Manchester Independent lines to the bottom right, burrowing by tunnel under the North Junction, and on the left the North Shed site. The hip-roofed building is the new signalbox, and it stands just about where the Middle Shed stood, the cars in the foreground are where the Outdoor Machinery Workshops were, and beyond the first set of railway lines (the Chester line), can be seen the site of the Old Works. The Heritage Centre stands in the apex between that line and the lines north.
*Gavin Morrison*

**Right:**
After World War 1 a memorial plaque was mounted at both North and South Sheds, to commemorate those members of the staff who had made the supreme sacrifice, and laid down their lives for King and Country. Out of the 300 North and South Shed men who took up arms, no less than 46 gave their lives in that terrible carnage. The North Shed plaque was mounted outside the shed on the District Office wall, and indeed could be seen from the station as well as from passing trains. The South Shed plaque — they were identical — was inside the shed, on the wall side of No 1 road. After World War 2 an additional plaque was mounted below the originals, listing the six men who also gave their lives for their country. These two beautifully-made bronze plaques were always kept highly polished, and the former South Shed one is seen here, now mounted in the entrance hall to the footplate staff booking-on point at Crewe station; I never have discovered what happened to the North Shed plaque.
*Gavin Morrison*

# 3
# South Shed

The extensive 1896-1904 remodelling plans for Crewe necessitated demolition of the old No 1 Shed at Crewe North. To replace this building, but equally important, to fit in with the proposed improvements at Crewe, and the segregation as far as possible of freight from passenger traffic, a new shed was built south of the station which naturally became known as Crewe South. The remodelling of Crewe included extensions to the already large marshalling yards at Basford Hall, and the division of up and down traffic into separate, albeit adjacent yards, both of which were to have their own individual shunting humps. A large transhipment shed was also brought into use in February 1901 and this, one of the largest of its kind, greatly speeded the transhipment of part wagon load traffic; it

was a model of its type when built, and remained so for years, placing the LNWR in the forefront of this sphere of railway activity.

Integral with the plan was the construction of a series of Independent lines, designed to keep the goods and mineral traffic clear of the station area, and in doing so allowed room for a considerable improvement to the passenger facilities. It was the construction of new Independent lines connecting Basford Hall with Crewe North Junction, and intended for traffic heading along the North Wales coast line, along with the passenger station enlargements, that caused the need to demolish the No 1 Shed at Crewe North.

The Independent lines, which are still termed as such today, were intended to serve the new marshal-

ling yards, as well as allowing through goods and mineral trains to bypass the station area. They left the main lines 1 mile 850yd south of Crewe South Junction, at what became Basford Hall Junction. Skirting the marshalling yards to the west, they formed a double triangular junction with the Shrewsbury line at Sorting Sidings South and Salop Goods Junction respectively. Then in a deep cutting, almost alongside and west of the station, they dived into a series of tunnels that took them under Crewe North Junction, to emerge and rejoin the main lines north, and the Manchester lines respectively.

Below:
**Crewe South in 1910, from the Third Edition 25in Ordnance Survey map.**

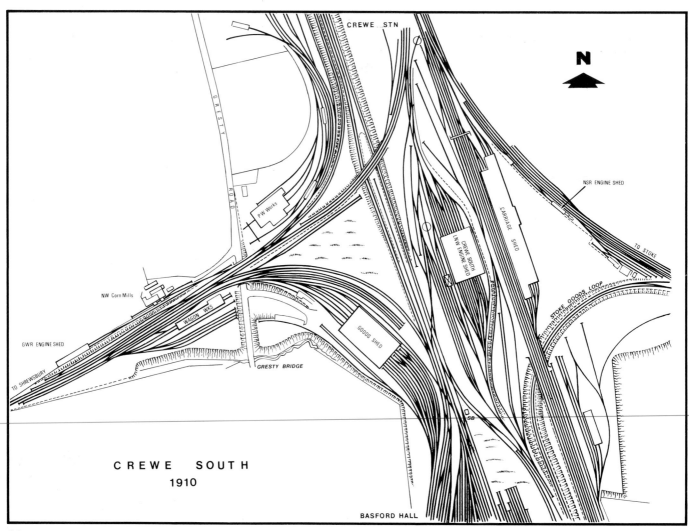

CREWE SOUTH
1910

Clearly, notwithstanding the need to demolish the No 1 Shed at Crewe North, there were distinct advantages to be had if locomotives involved in goods and mineral train working along with the marshalling yard shunters, did not have to travel backwards and forwards to Crewe North for servicing, etc; the lines were already congested with train movements, without a series of light engines too.

A new depot was planned and built in the space between the marshalling yards and Crewe South Junction, and sandwiched between the main line south, and the new Independent lines. Thereafter, Crewe South Shed traditionally housed the goods engines, with Crewe North looking

after the more prestigious passenger power, and locomotive allocations over the years echoed this strategy. The new depot was very well laid out as the site was far less cramped than that of the North Shed. It benefited from being designed as one integral unit from the start, rather than added to piecemeal over the years. The actual building was 273ft × 184ft, containing 12 full-length roads, a through-type shed with all roads having access from both ends; it was of the then standard Webb Northlight pattern. An extremely light and airy building in comparison with its North Shed counterparts, it was nevertheless an extremely draughty place, as most double-ended sheds tend to be. Alongside the eastern wall were the

Top:
**Newly-built and awaiting completion of the trackwork, Crewe South Shed is seen here in 1896, looking north. Notice the Webb Northlight pattern roof, doors to the shed, and the amenity block, office and workshops running parallel to the right-hand side of the shed — its east side. The coaling stage and water tank are to the left, with the Shrewsbury line on the embankment in the distance.**
*Crown Copyright/National Railway Museum Collection (CR A325)*

Above:
**Another view of the southern end of the new shed, taken at the same time as the previous one, and showing the run-round road, and the end of the mess room. Notice the engine preparation pits outside the shed on each road.**
*Crown Copyright/National Railway Museum Collection (CR A324)*

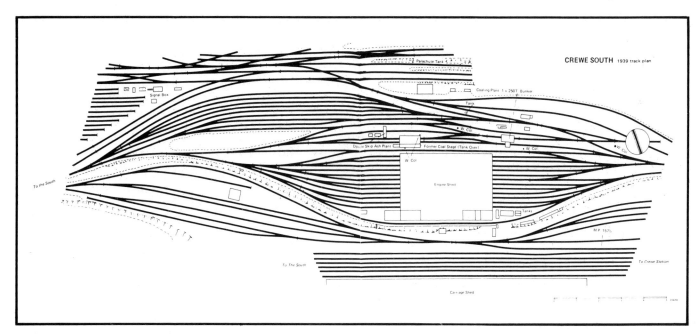

offices at the northern end, work-shops in the centre, with the mess rooms, other staff facilities and stores, towards the southern end. Around the time of World War 1, this amenity block was extended south-wards, thus becoming longer than the main shed building itself. Run-round roads were provided on both sides of the shed, with the traditional LNWR-type coaling stage to the west, along with ash pits etc. The water tank was, as usual, on top of the coaling stage, and to the north of the shed, towards Crewe South Junction, where separate inlet and outlet roads existed, was a 50ft turntable; there appears to have been a turntable here before the shed was built, and it seems that this was the table used for the shed. It is shown on the 1875 Ordnance Survey map. Despite access being provided at the South Junction the depot yard was laid out

so that the principal movements of locomotives on and off the shed were at the southern end of the yard, and to and from the marshalling yards. Indeed, separate Independent engine lines existed between the shed and Basford Hall Junction for that very purpose, so that light engine move-ments did not foul the running lines.

West of the shed was a fan of eight sidings, and these were used for the storage of locomotive coal, a small stocking ground being laid out alongside them. They were also used in later years to stable locomotives awaiting attention in Crewe Works,

Right:
**This photograph was probably taken during the 1921 strike, and looks south from Sorting Sidings Middle, showing many rows of stored locomotives. The main line south is on the extreme left, and Sortings Sidings South signalbox can be seen in the distance.**
*Collection Harry Newbiggin*

Below right:
**An interesting view taken in 1929 from the top of the coaling plant at the South Shed and looking south, towards the Marshalling Yards. The shed building is to the left, and the coal stage is in the foreground. Notice the stored loco coal, and the main line to the extreme left.**
*Collection Harry Newbiggin*

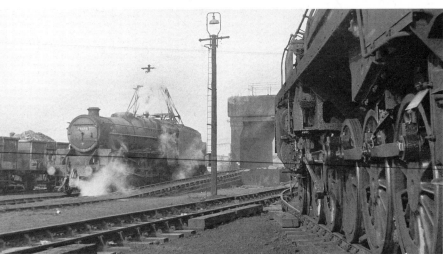

Above right:
**A view of the South Shed before World War 1, showing its northern end, with the coal stage just visible to the extreme right. The fine array of LNWR motive power includes, from left to right: a 'Super D' 0-8-0 freight engine; a 'Benbow' rebuild of a Webb compound; a 'Bill Bailey' 4-6-0; an 'Experiment' 4-6-0, with an early 0-8-0 freight engine behind it; another 'Super D', with a 'Precursor' class 4-4-0 alongside it, and finally what looks like a 'Precedent' class 2-4-0 passenger engine.**
*Collection A. G. Ellis*

Right:
**A 1967 view of Class 5 No 44675 leaving the old coal stage, whilst a Standard '9F' 2-10-0, No 92078, stands on the right. Notice behind the Class 5 the ash handling plant, and the wagons of ash, 5 February 1967.** *Dave Donkin*

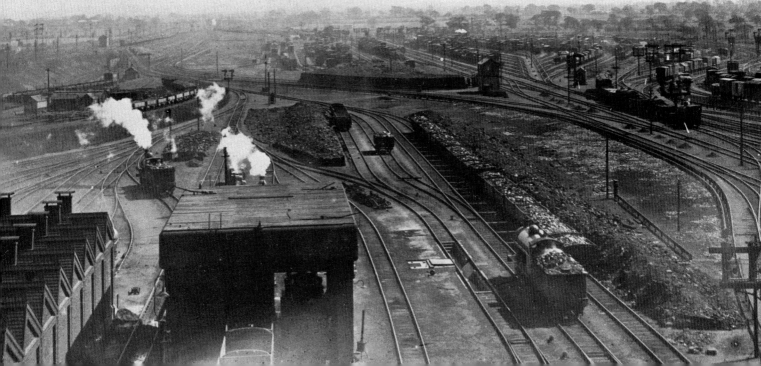

Above:
The southern end of the shed, showing engines stabled on the run-round road, and the extension of the buildings along the eastern wall. Main line at higher level to right, and Carriage Shed beyond that, 5 February 1967. *Dave donkin*

Left:
Class 5 No 44675 from Carlisle Kingmoor, under the old LNWR coal stage on 5 February 1967. Notice the elevated right-hand road, where the coal wagons would have stood.
*Dave Donkin*

Above right:
A busy scene at the coaling plant on 4 March 1967, showing 'Britannia' No 70024 (formerly *Vulcan*), about to take on coal, with another member of the class, No 70051 (formerly *Firth of Forth*) alongside. Notice that this locomotive is fitted with one of the coal-pusher tenders; view looks north.
*Dave Donkin*

Right:
One of the famous ex-LNWR 'Super D' 0-8-0 goods engines, this particular example, No 49125, being fitted with a tender cab, and glistening in the autumn sunshine on 21 October 1961. It appears to be just ex-works, awaiting to return to its home shed of Bescot. Although that shed became the last home of the class, they had been regular occupants of Crewe South from the day the shed was first built. *Gavin Morrison*

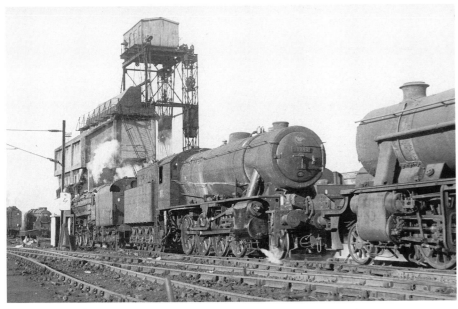

machine tools. However, a decision had to be made to close one or other of the sheds. This came out in favour of keeping Crewe South at the expense of Crewe North, and we saw in the previous chapter how the North Shed closed in 1965. It is interesting to speculate, however, if the North Shed might not have survived had its fabric been in better condition, because even in 1965 it was known that steam would only have between two to three years more life; but there must have been much pressure to close the North Shed and vacate the site, on environmental grounds alone. It was very close to the town, whilst the South Shed was well isolated from any domestic property. Before the South Shed could take on its increased repair role, much work needed to be done, including renovation of the wheeldrop, which had not worked for many years, and this piece of equipment, despite being of the newer hydraulic type, relied on a steam driven pump to maintain the hydraulic water pressure. There was a large vertical fire tube boiler in the workshop, and this powered the Scotch crank-type steam driven pump which was alongside it; all this had to be overhauled before it could be used, and I recall that the boilersmiths had to retube the boiler. On completion, it must have been the only steam-driven wheeldrop for miles . . . ! Of course, thereafter, it was necessary to give the steam raisers adequate notice, so that they could raise steam before any wheeldrop work could be undertaken; it was an amazing arrangement for the mid-1960s which never ceased to command my attention.

The wheeldrop at the North Shed was old, but this was something else . . . ! Presumably, many of the old LNWR sheds had had similar equipment, because both the drop table itself and the steam engine bore the unmistakable signs of having been built at Crewe, and the North Shed arrangement only differed in having had the steam engine and boiler removed, and replaced by an electric motor driven pump and hydraulic accumulator.

Rather than move the old machine tools from the North Shed, or renovate the even older equipment still in existence at the South Shed, it was decided to utilise the almost unused gear installed at the Diesel Depot (see Chapter 7) and therefore the axle box turning lathe, general-purpose centre lathe and shaper were moved and installed in the South Shed machine shop. Much equipment was brought from the North Shed, including cop-

persmiths' and whitemetallers' hearths and other sundry items. As there was no axle journal turning lathe, it became necessary that whenever wheels needed their journals turning, they had to be sent to the Works for attention. In the old days any wheels removed at the South Shed and needing turning would have been sent to the North Shed. But as it was known that this was only to be for a few years, it was not considered worthwhile to install a journal lathe. Timescales were such that all this work was not complete when the North Shed officially closed its doors on 24 May 1965, and it was necessary to retain some facilities there until the South Shed became self-sufficient in October. Mileage examinations and wheeldrop work continued to be carried out at Crewe North for a further five months after official closure. It was October too, before the breakdown train and crane were transferred, as the bulk of the staff who manned this equipment by this time tended to be employed on the type of work which was retained at the North Shed. However, the crane lost its undercover accommodation, and thereafter had to live outside with the remainder of the train in the sidings to the south of the South Shed. There had existed for some years a small breakdown facility at the South Shed, consisting of one combined riding and tool van

and a box van for additional packing; this would attend the smaller derailments in the marshalling yards, and save time in having to otherwise call out the North Shed gang.

The last few years of steam at Crewe proved to be both very busy and interesting, as the depot, perhaps somewhat surprisingly, took on more

Below:
The Crewe Cowans Sheldon 50-ton steam breakdown crane No 1005/50, seen here on 8 September 1967, standing in the sidings to the south of the South Shed. This crane had been at Crewe since 1939, and was transferred from the North Shed when it closed in 1965. Fitters David Owen — left — and Harry Morton can be seen on the crane, and the Carriage Shed is the building to the right, the diesel shunter just visible is engaged in shunting the Permanent Way pre-assembly depot. *Allan Baker*

Right:
The conditions under which steam locomotives were repaired at depots often left much to be desired, especially for the mechanical staff. This picture taken on 5 February 1967 shows very clearly such conditions. Class 5 No 44681 is undergoing a valve and piston examination out in the open, and Fitter Alf Dean and his mate are seen disconnecting the eccentric rod. Note the cylinder and valve chest covers on the floor, pressure relief valve on the step, and the 14lb hammer beneath it. The engine stands on No 2 road at the south end, and had been on Crewe's allocation for many years, being transferred to the South Shed on closure of the North. *Dave Donkin*

Below right:
The shed from the west on 29 September 1963, showing from left to right: the Carriage Shed, the shed itself, mechanical coaling plant, and finally the original coal stage with water tank on top. The line-up of stored engines in the foreground are, from the left, Nos 42981, 42983, 42947 and 44592. The track in front of them gave direct access from the southern end of the shed yard to the turntable. *F. W. Shuttleworth*

Above:
**After the closure of the former GWR shed at Gresty Lane, Western Region locomotives made more frequent visits to Crewe South; here is 'Grange' class 4-6-0 No 6878 *Longford Grange* at the south end of the shed yard on 29 February 1964.** *Dave Donkin*

Below:
**Another Western Region locomotive at the South Shed, this time 'Castle' class No 7023 *Penrice Castle*, awaiting a job to return it to its home shed of Shrewsbury. Photograph taken on 15 November 1964.** *Dave Donkin*

and more work. Due to the rundown in steam overhauls by Crewe Works, the depot found itself having to perform tasks that it had never been called on to do before, in the quest to keep locomotives in traffic long after their normal overhaul periods. For example, complete sets of superheater flues were renewed, a job never before undertaken at the sheds, except perhaps for the odd flue here and there. As the works ran down its facilities, and especially after the complete cessation of steam repairs, much equipment was acquired to

make the work easier. Prior to this, for example, the small number of tubes renewed at the sheds could easily be expanded into position by hand expanders, but it was an extremely laborious process completely to retube locomotive boilers day in and day out. Hence the air-operated expanding equipment was amongst the gear acquired. Not only South Shed-allocated locomotives benefited from this improvement in equipment; locomotives came from far and wide to have jobs of this nature performed on them.

With the final demise of steam at Crewe, the South Shed closed officially on and from Sunday 6 November 1967, but there were a number of odd steam workings for the next few weeks. For example, I noted 'Britannia' Pacifics Nos 70024 and 70025 in steam, having been left at

Above right:
**'Britannia' No 70025, like all its sister locomotives, shorn of its nameplates by this date, but formerly *Western Star*, is seen here on No 9 road on 8 September 1967, just a couple of months before the shed closed to steam in November. Fitters David Owen — left — and Harry Morton stand alongside her.** *Allan Baker*

Right:
**'Britannia' No 70014, standing on No 12 road at the northern end of the depot, awaiting a turn to take it back to its home shed of Carlisle Kingmoor on 14 January 1967. Notice the steam breakdown crane stabled on the road between the shed wall and the old coal stage. This was not its normal home.** *Martin Welch*

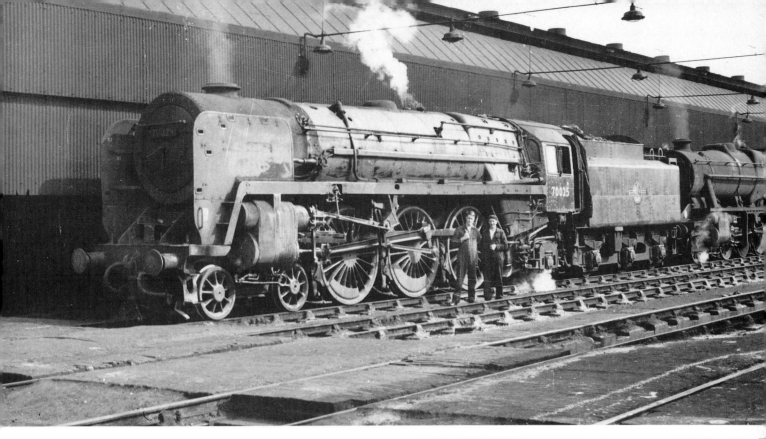

the shed after closure, being despatched to their home depot at Carlisle on 7 November. Likewise, Class 5 4-6-0s Nos 44878 and 45447 were similarly steamed to go home to Springs Branch on 8 November. Class 9F 2-10-0 No 92203 actually arrived under its own steam that same day, having come from Birkenhead after being bought privately for preservation by David Shepherd, and coming to Crewe for storage prior to delivery. On the eve of closure the actual allocation had been reduced to just six locomotives; Class 8F 2-8-0s Nos 48018, 48336, 48351, 48402 and 48729, together with Class 5 No 45145. The last employment for these engines were the coal

trains to and from Silverdale and Holditch collieries, both on the former North Stafford section, and by this time reached by the spur line that connected the old Newcastle-under-Lyme to Market Drayton line, to the West Coast main line at Madeley, a few miles south of Crewe. Also, nominally, on the Crewe allocation was privately preserved former London & North Eastern Railway (LNER) Pacific No 4498 *Sir Nigel Gresley*, still used occasionally for special workings.

Of the remaining engines '8Fs' Nos 48336, 48351 and 48729 were steamed on 16 November, and transferred away under their own steam that day. Likewise, Standard Class 5

No 73035 accompanied them, returning home to its own shed at Patricroft, having been stopped at Crewe South 'waiting material' on closure of the shed to steam. As late as 5 December, I noted '8F' No 48200 in steam on the shed, before departing for the marshalling yards on a down freight at about 09.00; but by then these were isolated examples.

No 4498 remained until 12 March 1968, when it left under its own steam and No 92203 — together with Standard Class 4 4-6-0 No 75029, which had also been bought by David Shepherd and which had been on Crewe's allocation — left under their own steam, and after a few minor repairs had been undertaken, on 4 April 1968. The last steam visitor of all was 'Britannia' Pacific No 70013.

This was the last steam locomotive to have been overhauled at a BR workshop — it had left Crewe Works after a general repair on 2 February 1967 — and visited Crewe Works for a final repaint prior to the last series of railtours before steam's final hour. It came off Crewe Works on the evening of Friday 19 June 1968 and left for its home shed of Carlisle, light engine, on the morning of Saturday 20 June. This locomotive had the distinction of being used on the last steam train run by BR, on 11 August 1968 to mark the end of steam traction.

Left:
**Another picture of Class 5 No 45145, on 17 November 1967. It apparently belonged to Holyhead. On the left is Fitter Harry Morton, with the author in the centre, and Fitter's Mate, the late Jack Hough, to the right.** *Allan Baker*

Top right:
**'Britannia' No 70013 *Oliver Cromwell* makes a splendid sight on the South Shed having recently emerged from the Works on 5 February 1967. This was on completion of the last works overhaul given to a steam locomotive for service use by any BR works, and the locomotive was specially painted in the fully lined livery, indeed it had carried its nameplates for the small ceremony held in the Works earlier in the day, but they had quickly been removed for safe keeping. Prior to its withdrawal from service at the end of steam operation, this locomotive participated in the last special train on 11 August 1968, and has subsequently been preserved at Bressingham in Norfolk.** *Dave Donkin*

Right:
**The author to the right, with his contemporary Chris Jones, seen in front of Class 5 No 44759 at Crewe South on 27 October 1967, just a couple of weeks before the end of steam operations at Crewe.** *Allan Baker*

After closure to steam, diesels continued to be stabled on the South Shed, and the footplatemen continued to book on and off there. However, a scheme was under way to commission new facilities for footplatemen to book on and off duty, with mess rooms etc, on Crewe station. This was not only for the South Shed crews, but the former North Shed men too. Old offices situated on the island Platform Nos 1-2 were refurbished, and came into use during the summer of 1968, the South Shed men transferring to them, along with the erstwhile North Shed men who, it will be recalled, had in the meantime been housed at the Bungalow. The South Shed itself did not long outlast the departure of its men, being demolished during the week ending 2 August 1968, and thereafter the yard was cleared up, some lighting installed, and freight diesels continued to be stabled there at what became known as Crewe South Holding Sidings. In an effort to improve the disjointed stabling facilities for diesel locomotives at Crewe (it will be recalled that many were still stabled on the North Shed site) a scheme was developed to combine the North and South facilities, alongside the Diesel Depot, in what was called the Old Yard, or sometimes referred to as the Down Yard. Full details of these plans will be found in Chapter 7.

To my mind Crewe South never had the character of the North Shed and always seemed to be looked on somewhat disparagingly by the North

Top right:
**The South Shed enginemen's barracks in Gresty Road, seen here on 4 February 1970. Notice the extensions to the right which date from World War 2. This building is still in existence, although it ceased to be used for its original purpose when lodging turns ceased in 1968.** *Allan Baker*

Centre right:
**View looking north along Platform 2 of the station on 15 June 1985, and showing, to the left, the offices where the train crew accommodation is now situated. This was after the former North and South Shed footplatemen were combined, and the offices came into use for this purpose in 1968.**
*L. A. Nixon*

Right:
**The South Shed War Memorial plaque, inside the shed and on the wall alongside No 1 road. This was remounted at the footplatemen's signing-on point on the station, after closure of the shed.**
*Collection Harry Newbiggin*

60

Shed men. I suppose this was not unnatural, in view of the latter's more prestigious activities in connection with its passenger power allocation, and of course, being the Headquarters of the Area. There seemed to be little interchange of maintenance staff between the two sheds, although the footplatemen had a common seniority between the two, and progressed through the links of both sheds. For the artisan staff however, one started as either a 'North Shed man' or 'South Shed man', and one remained so! My own personal experiences at Crewe South were much less than at the North, but we used to visit occasionally to help out, particularly during the last couple of winters of the North Shed's life, when with the reduction in the passenger steam allocation the amount of work to be done was often very small. We would undertake the odd X examination, 7-9 week periodic examination or whatever. Later, after I went to the Diesel Depot we would make occasional forays to the South Shed, either to visit the canteen (no such establishment existed at the Diesel Depot), or to repair the diesel shunters that were stabled there.

Entering the shed from the north, and alongside No 1 road, of the buildings on the eastern wall of the shed, first came the offices, which included the booking-on point, Running Foreman's office, general office and the Shedmaster's accommodation. Next came the workshop area, where the boiler and engine for the wheel drop were located, followed by the stores and Mechanical Foreman's office. Last of all came the canteen and staff amenities, with the former probably dating from World War 2, but it could have been earlier as it was located in the extension of the amenity block mentioned earlier. A new staff amenity block, consisting of toilets, locker room, wash room etc, had by this time been built to the east of the shed, and there were various other huts dotted around the site, to house fitters and their mates, boilersmiths and all the other shed grades, each seeming to require, and therefore develop, their own 'shanty towns', so typical a part of almost any steam locomotive depot anywhere!

Left:
**View of the shed yard looking southeast on 14 January 1967, and showing 'Britannia' No 70016 taking water. The overhead line equipment to the right was not energised, but erected at minimum clearance and was intended to ensure locomotive tenders were not coaled in excess of the loading gauge when leaving the shed.** *Martin Welch*

Below:
**Another view, also on 14 January 1967, looking southeast with the 70ft turntable in the foreground.**
*Martin Welch*

# 4
# Life at Crewe North

Working in a steam locomotive shed is an experience that anybody who has ever sampled is unlikely to forget; the experiences are difficult adequately to describe to others who have not been so fortunate. They were fantastic places, albeit very often dismal, dingy and extremely dirty. But to one such as myself, whose life-long interest had been in railways, and particularly loco-motives, they held a mystique impos-sible properly to recapture in the written word, no matter how persua-sive one's literary expertise. I recall vividly my first day at work, when only a few weeks after my 15th birthday, I took the train from Etruria, near my home in Newcastle-under-Lyme, to Crewe, and made my way — with not a few butterflies in my stomach — along Platform 1, over the footbridge and on to the North Shed. After the usual formalities, introduc-tion to the Shedmaster, Geoff Sands, and in the care of the kindly chief clerk, I was handed over to the tender mercies of Leading Fitter Bill Webb.

Right:

**If 'Duchess' No 46229 *Duchess of Hamilton* was not the most famous member of the class before withdrawal, it has certainly become so since its return to working order on 10 May 1980, under the auspices of the National Railway Museum. Built in 1938 it was the locomotive selected to tour the United States with the 'Coronation Scot' train the following year, and due to the outbreak of war remained there until 1942. For this trip it exchanged identities with the original member of the class, No 6220, but the two engines reverted to their correct identities on the return of No 6229. This locomotive's allocation alternated between Camden and Crewe North, until it was finally withdrawn on 15 February 1964, and purchased by Billy Butlin for display at his Holiday Camp at Pwllheli in North Wales. It is seen in these two illustrations after restoration to something like its earlier condition by Crewe Works, and on the North Shed on 18 April 1964. The photographs show the locomotive on No 4 road inside the Middle Shed, which by this date was one of the roads normally used for diesel servicing, and in one of the views a number of diesels can be seen. Notice also the Engine Arrangements board, and the generally poor condition of the shed roof — by this time 99 years old!**
*Gavin Morrison*

By this time the Middle Shed at Crewe North — it took me ages to discover why it was so called, when it was not in the middle of anywhere — was getting extremely decrepit, much of the roof being rotten and leaky, indeed bordering on dangerous in places. However, it was a wonderful place with tremendous character and a great group of workmates. At my tender age, I found Crewe people generally somewhat coarser than the extremely friendly Pottery people, with whom I had been brought up, but I very soon discovered that, deep down, folk from that part of Cheshire were kindly souls, and I came to know and love that part of the world second only to my native North Staffordshire. I can honestly say that I have never since worked with such a great bunch of people. It is often said that one's school days were the best days of one's life; not so in my case, but I can say without fear of contradiction that I enjoyed the years of my apprenticeship tremendously, and look back on them as among the most enjoyable.

The North Shed was reached from the offices and booking-on point, via an unlit inclined foot tunnel about 50ft long which passed through the southern end of the shed, between offices, mess rooms and stores. Once inside the shed, the 12 roads presented themselves in a fantastic vista to the young enthusiast embarking on his first day as a railwayman; was I going to get paid for this too? It was like a dream come true, for in

countless train spotting forays at Crewe, the North Shed was extremely difficult to gain entry to, and I had only once before penetrated its depths. Among the engines whose front ends were facing me was ex-LMS Pacific No 46253 (always plain 6253; I soon discovered that, unlike enthusiasts, railwaymen never used the initial '4' when referring to locomotive numbers); it stood at the end of No 8 road and was undergoing a No 8 Valve and Piston examination — (a V&P) — and became the very first locomotive I worked upon. I can see her now, as clear as on that Monday morning over 27 years ago.

What an amazing place this was; engines, both steam and diesel, a breakdown crane, 'shadow' boards full of all sorts of tools, benches, offices, workshops, machine tools, a drop pit, shear legs, tool lockers and lots of people going about their daily business; so much to take in all at once. The Middle Shed was a big shed, and was well equipped with all the machinery and gear necessary for a 'concentration' depot under the former LMS motive power 'engine maintenance and repair scheme', and it could handle a large fleet of locomotives. Along with its own allocation, which had generally hovered at around 110 locomotives for years, engines from the other sheds in the Crewe Motive Power District came to the North Shed for their larger examinations and repairs. Crewe North also undertook all the

No 8 V&P examinations on the entire fleet of LMR-allocated Pacifics, only Polmadie on the Scottish Region, did not send its Class 8 passenger engines to Crewe for this work to be done.

Bill Webb was a kindly soul, one of three leading fitters — Burt Ashwin and Tommy Brooks were the other two — who covered the three shifts, and who reported to a day turn mechanical foreman, a salaried grade, and at the time one Bill Short. He in turn reported directly to the Shedmaster, Geoff Sands, an Eastern Region-trained man who came to Crewe North having held a similar position at Stoke-on-Trent, but who had previously been in charge at far away Melton Constable, the former headquarters of the erstwhile Midland & Great Northern Joint Railway. Geoff went to the Southern Region at Basingstoke on promotion after leaving Crewe, but was later to forsake a very promising railway career to become Curator of Alan Bloom's Museum at Bressingham, and thereby remain closely associated

Below:
**Unfortunately it has not proved possible to locate a photograph of the Engine Arrangements board at either Crewe North or South, but as they were such an important part of shed life, it is considered that this view of the board at Newton Heath will not go amiss to illustrate the point; it is believed to have been one of the biggest such boards in the country.** *Collection Harry Newbiggin*

with his first love — the steam locomotive — and return to his beloved and native Norfolk. Tragically, Geoff died 'in harness' at Bressingham in 1976; it was a great loss for the preservation movement, and personally for me because, doubtless without his advice, I might never have taken the course I did in my railway career. Norman Peech, an imposing figure to my tender eyes, was the District Locomotive Superintendent who nevertheless always had a greeting: his headquarters were at the North Shed, and his assistant was Tom Vickers.

After showing me the extremely primitive (even by early 1960s standards) messing and cloakroom facilities, Bill Webb introduced me to Fitter Alf Platt, with whom I was to work over the next few months. Alf was quite a character and had been a Crewe railwayman and North Shed fitter for all of his working life. He would have been about 62 at the period I write of, and in his day had played professional football for Crewe Alexandra (the 'Alex', as the team was colloquially and affectionately referred to). Unfortunately, by this time Alf had a skin ailment, which was aggravated by contact with any form of oil, so his duties principally consisted of overhauling the piston valves of locomotives undergoing V&P examinations. Traditionally, he had the youngest apprentice with him and whenever we got jobs involving oil or grease, which was usually the case on a steam engine, I had to do most of the work! But this, of course, was great, and the very best way to learn.

Alf was an extremely thorough, competent and knowledgeable tradesman, and with him jobs were always done properly. There was never any corner cutting, or worse, 'bodging', with Alf, and it was a pleasure to watch him examine the piston valve heads for any fractures after they had been cleaned, and before they were re-ringed ready for replacement in the locomotive. I very soon learnt the knack of retaining the rings compressed into their grooves, so that the complete valve could be replaced in its liner easily, especially the rearmost head which, of course, could not be seen. Bits of Alf's old Woodbine packets were wedged between ring and groove, keeping the ring in compression. Of course, once the superheated steam hit them, the cardboard would burn away, and the rings would expand. I learnt a lot of the basic fitting skills with Alf; how to use a hammer and chisel without hitting one's knuckles all the time, how to recut valve seatings, how to make steamtight joints, the art of swinging a 14lb hammer and the like. The latter was, indeed an art, and one I have to say that I never fully mastered, and there were always plenty of guys better at it than I. It was amazing how much 'big hammer' work there was on a steam locomotive, and there were some real masters of the craft at Crewe North.

They had to be agile contortionists too, because some of the places where the hammer had to be swung were very cramped, for example inside motions, and getting a direct blow on the crosshead to piston rod cotter of outside motions. To achieve this was a three-man job, one would hold the dolly on the cotter, and this entailed crouching under the slide bars, another would be in the pit supporting the other end of the dolly, whilst the third swung the hammer. With the very shallow pits, the latter was no easy task, and it was necessary to develop skills so as to be able to bend one's arms inwards to avoid the pit bottom during the swing, and then outwards again to give maximum power as the hammer struck the dolly; it was extremely difficult. Imagine then, a timid 15-year-old, crouching in the pit supporting a heavy dolly, with a fellow brandishing as big a hammer as I had ever seen, doubled up against one side of the pit; it was frightening to say the least, but I soon learnt how important it was to trust the fellow with the hammer as they knew exactly what they were doing and never missed, and to hold the dolly very loosely, or hands and arms stung for hours!

At the time, Nos 1 and 2 roads of the Middle Shed had been foreshortened to around two thirds of their original length, and this had allowed construction of a canteen and pay office, within the shed and alongside its eastern wall. The canteen opened in February 1943, and most depot canteens date from that period, as more and more enginemen had to spend longer periods away from their home sheds. Previously, this building had been the artisan staff mess room, and the leading fitters' office. No 3 road had also been shortened, not quite as much as the

others, and it ran parallel to the pay office and canteen for part of its remaining length. No 1 road was always kept to house the 50-ton Cowans-Sheldon steam breakdown crane, No RS1005/50, and this wonderful old crane (Cowans No 5111), had originally been built in 1930 as a 36-ton crane and allocated to Leeds Holbeck. In 1939, along with its two sisters (Cowans 5112-3, Nos RS1001/50 and RS1054/50), it was returned to its makers and modified to increase its lifting capacity to 50 tons at 18ft radius; thereafter it came to Crewe and remained until withdrawal in 1981.

For the last occasion with rail breakdown cranes built for use in this country, Cowans fitted six outriggers rather than four with three per side, and this made these cranes extremely stable in all circumstances, and helped facilitate the increase in their lifting capacity. Indeed, tales have been told of them lifting in excess of 75 tons! Other features were a lattice type articulated jib, and two four-wheeled weight-relieving bogies. At the time of writing, RS1054/50 is still in use at Haymarket Depot in Edinburgh, one of about three steam breakdown cranes still in use on BR; it has, however, now been withdrawn from service.

The exploits of this crane when at Crewe are legendary, and it attended all the major collisions on the Western Division of the LMS and later LMR from 1939 onwards, including such familiar names as Weedon, Penmaenmawr, Bourne End, Winsford, Minshall Vernon, Hixon, and the most infamous of them all, the carnage at Harrow. There were still men in the breakdown gang at Crewe when I started who had helped clear up the wreckage at Harrow, and the stories they could tell were horrific in terms of the damage caused, but fascinating in terms of the clearance operations. The crane was always kept in immaculate condition, specially painted in the same fully-lined maroon livery as the maroon Pacifics rather than the unlined lighter red of its lesser brethren, and it was kept in light steam all the time. It was the proud boast of Crewe North that at any time of the day or night, the breakdown train could be fully manned and away within half an hour of a call. When a call came, it was necessary to draw the crane out of the shed and unite it with the tool, jacking and riding vans, which were kept in Welsh's siding — I never did

discover how this siding got its name — it was one of the roads that ran alongside the eastern wall of the shed, and in this case extended to the road bridge that took the Nantwich Road over the railway.

Nos 2, 3, 4 and 5 roads were by this time used by the diesels, in the main English Electric Type 4s (later Class 40), and a few BR-Sulzer Type 4s (later Class 44 and 45), along with visiting 'Warship' diesel-hydraulics from the Western Region. A fuelling installation existed outside the shed and servicing, along with the daily examinations and the smaller repairs, were carried out. All the main line diesels allocated to Crewe North, and indeed all the others allocated to West Coast main line depots, had their larger examinations and all heavy repairs undertaken at the then quite new Diesel Depot, situated south of the station, and described in detail in Chapter 7.

Nos 6, 7 and 8 roads were used by engines having V&P examinations, especially at their southern ends, so that engines could be positioned with their smokeboxes towards the dead ends of the pits, making movement of component parts to and from the workshop much easier. There were generally two Pacifics undergoing V&P examinations at any one time, along with two or three locomotives of other types. No 9 road was almost completely boarded over and occupied by, from south to north: fitters' tool lockers, the Mechanical Foreman's office (this was a two storey fabricated type building, with the Clerk's office underneath and universally known as 'The Odeon', which probably dates it from the mid-1930s), work study office, and a storage area for firebox arch bricks and the like. No 10 road pit was similarly boarded over for around half its length, and was used for the storage of springs and other large components. No 11 road had the hydraulic wheeldrop at its midpoint, and it extended southwards beyond the others into the workshop, whilst No 12 road had at its southern end a pair of hydraulic shear lifting legs. These were large enough to lift many of the old LNWR passenger types, so that wheelsets could be removed, and 'Precursors' and 'George the Fifth' class engines had been so dealt with. However, I only saw them used for the Class 3F shunting tanks from Crewe South, and the odd diesel shunter; the wheeldrop to all intents and purposes reigned supreme for

such work. The use of hydraulic water power at Crewe was extensive, and in its day had been quite innovative. There was a pumping station and accumulator in the rearward extension of the Middle Shed, and among other things supplied power to the station lifts. The wheeldrop would operate and remove wheels from locomotives with pressure from the main supplied by these pumps, but to refit wheels it was necessary to use a small electrically-driven booster pump which was provided for this purpose. By the time I speak of this the pumping station had gone, but the booster pump was still there, and was needed for all wheeldrop activities.

The workshop was quite extensive, and certainly well-equipped. There was a belt-driven wheel lathe, which was not only capable of turning axle journals, but could also reprofile tyres, although I never saw it being used for the latter purpose. The axlebox lathe was very interesting, and I have never seen its like since, in that it had a drilling machine combined with its headstock. It was, I learned later, a standard provision under the LMS 'concentration' scheme. There was also a smaller general purpose centre lathe, shaping machine and equipment for white metalling crossheads, motion bushes and the like, together with the necessary presses, etc, coppersmiths hearth and sundry other items needed for the everyday maintenance and repair of steam locomotives. George Burton was the large and friendly, albeit sometimes cantankerous, coppersmith who 'lived' in this area. Direct access was available from the workshop area to Station Street, together with a small crane, and this enabled material to be loaded in and out of road transport, for conveyance to the Works as and when necessary.

Also at the southern end of the shed was locker accommodation for the footplatemen, rather primitive washing facilities for anybody, the leading fitters' and boilersmiths' office, fitters' lobby, footplatemen's mess room and stores. The latter was a large two storey building, integral with, and forming the south eastern corner of the shed but, due to their size, many large components like the springs already mentioned, had to be kept elsewhere. It was a constant battle for the stores people to keep tabs on material not actually in the stores, as somebody was always taking things without telling them. It was ever thus, I fear, and remains to this day even with more modern forms of motive power! Originally the large sand dryers were at the southern end of the shed, in the area later occupied by the leading fitters' office etc, but by my time they were situated at the southern end of what remained of Abba.

I eventually elucidated that this shed, described in Chapter 2, had been completed in 1868, the year Theodore, ruler of Amhara — part of Abyssinia — imprisoned some British officials. As a consequence, a force under the command of Sir Robert Napier invaded the country and Theodore was deposed, and after a period of civil war the country was reunited under the rule of Tigrê. This country (Ethiopia), has a long and fascinating history; suffice it to say here that presumably Sir Robert's victory over King Theodore at Magdala, for which he received a GCB and was raised to the peerage as Lord Napier of Magdala on 17 July 1868, caused so much interest in this country that its name was bestowed on this new shed. Indeed an Act of Parliament (Vic 31-2 Ch lxxxxi) received the Royal Assent on 31 July of that year, granting Sir Robert an annuity of £2,000, and his next surviving male heir, for the term of their natural lives; such was the gratitude of the country.

Abba was not parallel to the Middle Shed because of the route taken by Station Street, and in the apex between the two sheds was situated the Chargehand Cleaner's office, Fitters' cabin (formerly a tool store until the canteen was opened) and drying/cloak room, Brickarchman's facilities and toilets. The latter were extremely primitive, and one sat in full view of anybody who happened to pass that way! The fitters' cabin was an amazing place, with seating at benches alongside wooden aluminium-topped tables provided for about 24 people. A large and very old gas stove in one corner was home to an enormous cast iron kettle, which seemed to be constantly on the boil, and there was a brick fireplace. It was a function of the apprentices not only to keep this fire stoked in winter time, but also to maintain adequate supplies of coal easily to hand for the afternoon and night shifts, such supplies being piled high in an adjacent small locker room. Supplies were acquired by manhandling coal from the tenders of locomotives

'stopped' in the shed, and then by wheelbarrow to the cabin. Woe betide the apprentice who allowed either the fire to go out or stocks to run down! I have seen tremendous infernos alight in this most sacred of sacred places, and we all kept very warm during meal and tea breaks; we needed to be, because the shed was not only completely devoid of heating of any sort, but also without doors, and by this time, most of its roof too.

If the fitters' cabin was amazing, then the Brickarchman's accommodation can only be described as incredible, a mere shack cantilevered off the end of the cabin obviously home-made, and in which there was not even sufficient room to stand upright. There seemed no logical reason to me why these hardy souls should not have messed in the same place as the fitters and their mates, but they never did, and along with the tubers and boilermakers seemed a world apart. These latter two groups lived mainly in a small drying/cloakroom which was adjacent to the cabin, and a part of the same building; one only saw them in the cabin when filling their brew cans or the like.

It was in this apex between the two sheds that the ritual of decarbonising locomotives' blastpipes took place. At V&P examinations the blastpipe casting was removed to be cleaned of the build up of carbon, a result of the lubricating oil and superheated steam. The quickest and easiest way of performing this operation was to mount the casting on top of a couple of arch bricks, and then light a fire underneath it; the carbon would very soon ignite and merrily burn away until the blastpipe was as clean as the day it left the foundry. Of course, over-zealous stoking of the fire led young mischievous apprentices to vie

among themselves as to who could get the highest flame, and the reddest blastpipe; an operation often brought to an untimely end by intervention from some older spoil-sport, or so we thought!

Much of Abba had been demolished by the period I write of, to make way for a new semi-roundhouse, which only ever managed to reach about a third of its intended size, and was capable of housing but 12 locomotives on roads radiating from a 70ft turntable. However, four of Abba's roads remained under some form of roof remnants, with a fifth road that was no longer under cover. Such roof that did exist was generally in a worse condition than that over the Middle Shed, if this was possible! At the dead end of this shed was the Blacksmith's shop — a very necessary part of any establishment intended to maintain steam locomotives; Ernie Hilditch being the ever helpful blacksmith. Alongside this was a storage area used for arch bricks, firebars and other large items including fire irons and the sand dryers.

The adjoining semi-roundhouse was the only part of the shed to enjoy the luxury of doors, and it was a pleasant, light and airy building. Its main fault from a locomotive maintenance and repair point of view was the depth of its pits. It was not really practicable to undertake work on inside motions there and because the rails were not level with the shed

Below:
**One of the Caprotti valve gear Class 5 4-6-0s allocated to Llandudno Junction, in the semi-roundhouse at Crewe North in 1961. Notice that the rail head is not level with the shed floor, making outside motion removal difficult. No 44750 still sports the older BR logo on its tender.** *Neville Davies*

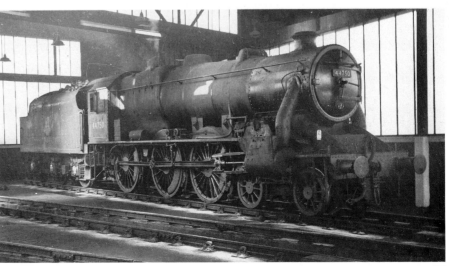

floor, and the chairs were exposed it was difficult to remove and replace outside motion parts. There was a lot to be said for the very shallow pits of traditional steam sheds, cramped that they might be, because steam engine parts are generally very heavy, and cumbersome. Of course, if some kind soul had dropped their fire, or if an especially dirty boiler had been washed out, then the older shallow pits often became unnegotiable when there was an engine standing over them. For these reasons very few mileage examinations or heavy repairs were undertaken in the round-house, but routine examinations and wash-outs were undertaken there. Generally however, it was reserved for engines in steam which were prepared there by their crews.

This is perhaps a good juncture to describe how springs were changed on a steam locomotive, and they all seemed to consume these components in prodigious quantities — to my young mind anyway — we always seemed to be changing them! First of all, in the case of coupled wheels, a check was made to see if the main spring buckle pin would clear the wheel spokes; if not the engine was moved until it would, either under its own steam if possible, or with a pinch bar. Then, after securing the locomotive from movement and scotching the wheels, a jack would be placed in a suitable place, and as much weight as possible taken off the offending spring by jacking up the engine. After this, depending on the type of fixture, the hangers would be disconnected. Older types of locomotive had screwed hangers, and it would be necessary to run-down the retaining nuts, noting exactly where they were originally so that they could be run back to the same place, so that the new spring would take its equal share of the weight; ideally, of course, after a spring change the locomotive should have been weighed, and the total load redistributed as necessary, thus allowing for differing spring tensions due to their respective ages. However, this was not usual practice at the sheds, as they did not have weighing facilities. No more was the instruction to renew the opposite spring ever followed to my knowledge!

The spring hanger nuts were often very tight, and there were many tubes available, enabling greater torque to be applied to the already very large spanners. I very soon developed some commendable muscles! Sometimes the nuts were so tight that the service of the blacksmith and his mate were called upon, and they would warm up the nut with an oxyacetylene flame; anti seize compounds did not seem to exist in those days. Sometimes even this failed, and the only cure was to split the nut with a cold chisel and hammer, an extremely laborious process. Once the hangers were free, a contraption

Below:
**'Royal Scot' No 46170 _British Legion_ had just emerged from its last visit to Crewe Works for overhaul when this photograph was taken inside the roundhouse, in 1961. Like No 46106, this locomotive also had unique features, in that it had been rebuilt from the high pressure locomotive No 6399 _Fury_, and had a different boiler from the remainder of the class; it became the prototype of the later general rebuilding of the 'Scots'. Being slightly heavier, this locomotive was more restricted on the routes it could cover, being prohibited on the former Midland main line for example, and its working life was therefore shared entirely between the main West Coast main line depots of Camden, Longsight and Crewe North. It was the first 'Royal Scot' to be placed in store, although neither the first to be officially withdrawn, or the first to be cut up. Going into store at Llandudno Junction on completion of the summer service of 1962, it was withdrawn, without having returned to service, in December 1962. The fitter appears to be tightening up a connection to the vacuum reservoir, no doubt attending to a vacuum leak.** _Neville Davies_

Right:
**A nice clean Class 5 No 45380, allocated to Edge Hill and here standing on one of the roads built to serve the new 70ft turntable, but before the semi-roundhouse was built. Picture taken on 20 August 1955. Notice the coal wagons standing on the site of the erstwhile Stock Shed, and the water tank.** _Brian Morrison_

Below right:
**The last 'Duchess' to be built by the LMS was appropriately named after its designer, _Sir William A. Stanier FRS_, and the locomotive is seen here on the 70ft turntable at Crewe North in 1962. Notice the roundhouse behind the locomotive; this was the last of the class to be withdrawn in October 1964, here it sports the later livery.** _The late George Wheeler_

After lunch it was the turn of the inside motion, one team splitting the crossheads whilst the other disconnected the big ends. These were dirtier and more difficult tasks, as room was at a premium, the shallow pits making the swinging of a 14lb hammer difficult, but they did make the actual dropping of the component parts much easier, and believe me those inside connecting rods, big end straps and brasses were heavy. By the end of the day pretty well all the motion parts would be stripped, and in the workshop for attention as necessary.

Tuesday morning would see any remaining motion parts needing attention removed, for example the rocker arms, expansion link guides, die block etc, together with the reversing gear, but these were only removed as and when they needed attention following examination. Only the rocker arms and their pivot bushes, together with the valve rods and combining levers, generally needed such attention on every locomotive. Any parts that required repairs in the Works would be despatched by road motor, direct to the shop within the Works complex that would be responsible, and the staff in the shed workshop would be busy pushing bushes out of the rods ready for remetalling, and subsequent turning; similarly the crossheads would be remetalled and remachined.

Many other jobs would now be undertaken whilst waiting for the motion parts to be returned, and the bushes etc remetalled. The blastpipe would be removed for decarbonising, the engine and tender would be split so that the intermediate drawgear could be examined, and renewed as necessary. All the axlebox underkeeps would be removed for examination of the journals, cleaning and renewal of the underkeep pads, and cleaning of the oil reservoir. Whilst this operation was underway all the oil connections from the mechanical lubricators would be disconnected, and the lubricators turned manually to pump the oil, and so ensure that all the pipes were clear. At this stage too, the opportunity would be taken to carry out an X day examination, and any other periodic examinations due.

Other items requiring attention during the V&P examination included the cylinder cocks, anti-vacuum valves, cylinder pressure relief valves, cylinder and valve chest bores and the valve rod guides, lubricator

drives, crank axle and the piston carriers. These latter were spring-loaded semi-circular bronze inserts, fitted into a recess at the bottom of the piston head, and between the rings. They were intended to take some of the weight of the piston, and thereby reduce ring wear. The piston rings themselves would be renewed, and the security of the piston head checked.

Wednesday would see the completion of these tasks, and any repairs arising, and the patient would start to be put together again. The pistons and crossheads would be replaced, along with the valves and all the covers. Removal and replacement of the inside crossheads was a difficult task, and it was usual to rig up a form of hoist around the boiler to ease the weight. These crossheads must have weighed all of 2cwt each, so the reader can imagine the difficulty in carrying out this job.

Thursday would see the outside motion going back, the engine and tender reconnected, blastpipe replaced, and the arrival of the parts that had been sent to the Works for attention. The inside connecting rods were usually the last parts to go back, and if all went according to plan the whole job would be complete by Friday lunchtime, or shortly after. Great care had to be taken in refitting the inside big ends, and ensuring they were a good 'running fit'. Each half brass had what we called a 'stink bomb' fitted in it, and these canisters contained a strong smelling liquid that gave off an odour similar to garlic. Very like a double ended shotgun shell, they were sealed by lead which, having a melting point slightly lower than the whitemetal of the bearing, was intended to allow the garlic smell to escape just prior to the overheating of a big end bearing. Thus, the driver would be warned. To remove these canisters, which were a tight fit in a hole bored in the half brass, concentric to the bearing surface itself, it was necessary to drive them out gently using a soft dolly; of course, this had to be done every time the brasses needed remetalling. I recall one over-eager contemporary of mine being a little too hard with the hammer, and, puncturing the lead, the shed did not smell right for weeks!

The Pacifics had a forked type inside connecting rod, with the brasses being retained by a cotter to the rear of the fork. However, it is interesting to note that the ex-LMS

three-cylinder engines had a different arrangement, with the brass retaining strap being separate from the rod, to which it was connected by two large bolts, which themselves went through a large boss at the end of the rod itself. The adjusting cotter passed between the brasses and the boss on the end of the rod. The three-cylinder BR Standard Pacific No 71000 had a similar arrangement to the LMS Pacifics.

When fitting the inside big ends, first of all it was necessary to offer the half brasses up against the journal, with a coating of engineers' blue over the whitemetal bearing surface, by then moving them to and fro, the accuracy of the fit could be determined by the amount of blue transferred to the journal. Of course, the actual diameter and 'running' clearance would have been determined beforehand by use of large callipers and a micrometer, but it would be necessary to scrape the radii at the edge of the brasses by hand, and where they fitted up against the web of the crank axle. This was a heavy and time-consuming process, to keep offering the heavy half brasses up and down in the pit, or taking them to and from the bench so that they could be hand scraped. Great care had also to be taken in making and fitting new felt oil pads, and in cleaning out the oil reservoirs in the rod ends, and checking the oil restrictors and trimmings. However, it has to be said that the inside big ends of the ex-LMS engines were remarkably trouble free, and cases of overheating were rare. Staff continually on this sort of work developed some commendable muscles, and it was a hard and heavy job, nonetheless interesting and absorbing to one such as me. I take great pride in having played just a little part in keeping these magnificent locomotives running.

There was usually a separate gang of men engaged on wheeldrop work, and they were led in my time by Fitter Les Lines, who was also the Leading Breakdown Fitter. He had a couple of regular mates with him, and they worked a day turn of duty. If an engine went on to the 'drop' for attention, provided it was a two-cylinder type, the offending wheelset would usually be out within a shift. The axleboxes would then be removed to be remetalled, and the wheelset placed in the lathe for the journal to be machined. The brass would subsequently be fitted to the

Above:
**Class 5 No 44860 is inside No 12 road of the Middle Shed, on 5 May 1963.**
*Mike Fell*

journal, before itself being fitted to the axlebox, and then the wheels would be placed back in the locomotive, the whole operation taking in the region of three days. Of course, in earlier times, when the incidence of hot boxes was greater, the wheeldrop would be manned on more than one shift, with a consequent reduction in the time taken to repair individual locomotives.

V&P examinations on other types of locomotives were quite often not as easy as the Pacifics, especially as the locomotives became more and more run down as the days of steam became numbered. Splitting crossheads and removing piston valves would be the most difficult part, as periods between removal increased. If the crosshead cotters were very tight, to ease their removal, and so that a more direct blow with a 14lb hammer could be achieved, one or other of the slide bars would be removed, so that the crosshead could be turned around, and the small end of the cotter hit directly, rather than via a cumbersome dolly from the pit. The use of oxyacetylene gear to

warm up the components was frowned upon, due to the possible problems of local heating, but often heat would be applied by the simple expedient of wrapping around the piston rod and crosshead a lot of rags well-soaked in paraffin, and then setting them alight; it is surprising how much heat can be generated this way, and it frequently did the trick. Naturally, the apprentices vied with each other as to who could get the largest inferno!

Once the cotter was out, it was still necessary to split the taper fit between piston rod and crosshead, and this too could result in a lot of heavy slogging. There were a number of the staff who had exceptional talents with 14lb hammers and were legendary in their power and ability to swing these instruments. If difficulty was being experienced they would be summoned one by one, in a previously defined pecking order, to try their hands and it was just not done to get those at the top end of the league, until lesser mortals had tried their hand. As I have already mentioned, it was a real art to get maximum power behind each blow, one I never mastered myself as I always seemed to 'strangle' the swing, by gripping the shaft of the hammer too near its head; but I never

ceased to be amazed and impressed when watching the masters at work.

Removing superheater elements was a dirty and disagreeable job, especially on a Monday morning with clean overalls due to last the week. It was the usual procedure to first get a strong water jet and wash out the interior of the smokebox of as much dirt and grime as possible before entering. Not only was it generally difficult to undo the nuts retaining the elements to the header, but sometimes it was no less awkward to remove the actual elements from the flues. All sorts of tactics were employed, including the not infrequent appropriation of an adjacent locomotive in steam! Even after removal, it was difficult to ensure a good steam tight joint when refitting, so that they would not continue to blow at the header joints after refitting. Blowing element joints caused loss of smokebox vacuum, so drivers would not hesitate to book them, but I often wondered if we achieved any lasting improvement by removing and refitting them. Very often the jointing faces were badly pitted, and whilst we could renew the coned jointing block from the elements themselves, there was little we could do with the mating surface on the header.

Working on engines in steam always excited me just that little bit more that is, Y scheme as opposed to X scheme in Crewe parlance. Steam locomotives, indeed steam engines of any sort, take on a completely new aura when in steam, and come alive to my mind. Of course, working on machines that get so hot can sometimes be difficult, but I used to enjoy renewing, say, a boiler gauge glass or a piston rod packing far more on an engine in steam than on a dead one. Some jobs were by no means so enjoyable, and it is difficult to think of one more awkward than renewing an exhaust injector on a locomotive in steam. This particular job would not normally be done in steam, but was occasionally if the offending piece of equipment was refusing to respond to all the known tricks to keep it working until the next X day. The job required much in the way of packing, pit planks, and levers of all sorts, shapes and sizes, as it was just about impossible to use any form of lifting appliance, the injectors on ex-LMS engines being under the footplate, and between engine and tender. Whilst undertaking the task, one would get frequent doses of hot water and steam down one's neck, and if the steam valve was blowing through at all, as they sometimes were, the whole thing would be very hot.

With the Y scheme work the leading fitter on each shift would visit the running foreman periodically and collect any repair cards deposited by drivers of incoming locomotives. He would then distribute them to the fitters, along with any cards detailing repairs found by the examining fitters, as they undertook their daily examinations. The fitter allocated the work would then visit the engine arrangement board, to see if and when the engines were booked out, and where they were stabled, thus allowing himself as much time as possible to carry out the repairs. Many and varied were the jobs undertaken on engines in steam, anything from a minor blow needing but a turn with a spanner, to the occasional removal of a piston valve that was blowing through, or the injector renewal already mentioned.

Particularly lousy jobs were problems with either rocking or drop grates, which often necessitated somebody going inside the firebox. Indeed, I have more than once been in the firebox of a locomotive in steam, albeit with the fire itself removed, wrapped up in all number of rags, to free a jammed rocker bar, drop grate or whatever. Directly one was out again, and the grate restored, fire from another locomotive would be placed in the box, the blower would be turned hard on, and the fire built up. As a 15-year-old I recall vividly being coaxed into my first firebox — on a dead engine on that occasion I hasten to add — by Alf Platt, but once I had been in and out a few times, it was child's play!

I could go on recalling experiences for much longer, but suffice it to say that I think, and indeed hope, that I have illustrated sufficient of the way of life in a steam shed for my readers to gain some knowledge of what it was all about. It was a great time for me, and I enjoyed it tremendously. We had some good laughs, as often mischievous apprentices are wont to. One recalls incidents like putting the water bags (this was a common Crewe term for a water hose) into a tender tank when one knew a fellow apprentice was inside attending to a broken water tank gauge or whatever! Or perhaps slamming a smokebox door shut, trapping a colleague inside, and then lighting a small fire in the firebox! Fortunately the thinner ones among us were able to extract ourselves via the chimney, but not everybody was so nimble. . . .

One last point is worthy of mention, and one that stands out in my mind as clearly as any other, especially in this very selfish world we seem to live in today. Such was the comradeship that when work was done for the day, we would all rally round any of our number who had still not completed their allotted tasks, and assist them until we were all 'straight up' — to use a Crewe term — and then we could all retire to the cabin for refreshments, or behind the roundhouse for a game of football, darts or whatever. This was, of course, well before the days of bonus schemes, and other such disincentives!

'Royal Scot' class 4-6-0 No 46157 *The Royal Artilleryman* at Crewe North on 7 August 1954. *J. E. Wilkinson*

# 5
# The 'Big Uns'

Lots could be written about Crewe's locomotive allocation over the years, especially that of Crewe North, and it would embrace almost every passenger locomotive the old LNWR ever owned, and all the principal passenger types introduced by the LMS. Indeed, many of the new Stanier types built at Crewe were first allocated to Crewe North, until they had been run in. All the LNWR passenger designs would have had their prototypes first allocated to Crewe, not only to be kept under observation by the Works staff, but also because Crewe North was responsible for so much of the main line work on the old North Western.

Crewe's strategic position gave its enginemen the widest route knowledge of any men on the system, and many of them would sign not only the West Coast main line between Euston and Carlisle, but also Birmingham, Manchester, Liverpool, Holyhead, Shrewsbury and Derby, to name just the major places. Later, under LMS auspices, Glasgow, Perth and Hereford would appear on their route cards. In more recent times, to compensate for the loss of the lodging turns to Glasgow and Perth, Cardiff has appeared! During World War 2 they even penetrated the Mid Wales line as far as Abergavenny.

Rather than expand on the fleets of locomotives and the activities of the men in general terms, I have decided to use one fleet of locomotives to illustrate in some detail what Crewe, its locomotives and men were all about, not least a class of locomotive on which Crewe men achieved their most legendary efforts. What better then, than to home in on the 'Big Lizzies'?

Much has been written over the years about Stanier's legendary Pacifics, and a plethora of volumes on them have appeared over the last few years. Readers of this book could therefore be forgiven if they assumed that just about all that could be said, had been said; but this is I suspect far from the case. Unfortunately, much of what has appeared in print recently, and many of the illustrations, are a repetition, or at best a regurgitation and reshuffling of what had gone before. In this chapter, therefore, I intend dealing with the subject rather differently, concentrating I hope, on hitherto less generally-known aspects, with a heavy emphasis on the activities of the Crewe North fleet, and the work undertaken on the locomotives at that shed.

It is generally helpful to a reader if an author states very clearly his prejudices and partisanships from the onset of his writings, so let me say right here and now that I consider the 'Duchesses' the finest express passenger locomotives ever built in this country. But I also consider myself sufficiently broadminded to accept the counter claims of others differently minded, and I hope that what I write about these locomotives here, will be accepted within that context.

Below:
**A nice 1953 line-up on the down through line at Crewe station, showing 'Duchess' No 46245 *City of London*, still with sloping smokebox front, a legacy of its earlier streamlining, and sporting the short-lived blue livery, reserved for the most powerful express passenger types. Behind it are Class 5 No 45163, and Class 4 tank No 42426. All look 'fresh off' works, and have no doubt been on a running in trip along the Shrewsbury line.** *Neville Davies*

William A. Stanier (later Sir William) had the ability of being able to form extremely clear practical ideas of profitable ways of advancement in engineering, utilising what was already best practice, and developing it into designs that were right first time. He was not, however, one to get too involved in the finer details of applying such ideas, and it was the association of Stanier and his Chief Draughtsman, Tom Coleman, that proved the winner that gave the Stanier designs the reputation they so richly deserved. Stanier's perceptions and Coleman's detail were the true ingredients that formed 'The mighty restocking of the LMS locomotive fleet', as O. S. Nock has so aptly referred to it.

Thomas F. Coleman was born in Endon, Stoke-on-Trent in 1874, the son of a schoolmaster, and he served his apprenticeship with the Stoke-based private locomotive builder, Kerr Stuart & Co Ltd, before joining the small, but much respected, NSR, as a draughtsman in 1905. Respected that is, by its bigger neighbours, including the mighty LNWR, a company that had tried unsuccessfully to swallow it up many times in the NSR's early years. Under J. H. Adams, Locomotive Superintendent of the NSR, Coleman progressed in the drawing office at Stoke Works and, among other achievements, was largely responsible for the famous wagon lift installed at his native Endon. This piece of equipment was

Below:
**Early signs of the electrification works are evident, as Carlisle Upperby 'Duchess' No 46226 *Duchess of Norfolk* takes the down 'Royal Scot' out of Platform 2 and on its way north, on 23 March 1959. The Crewe Arms Hotel can just be seen to the left of the locomotive, which would be working through between London and Carlisle.**
*Gavin Morrison*

Bottom:
**Crewe North 'Big Un' No 46252 *City of Leicester* negotiating the complicated layout at Glasgow Central, as it prepares to couple on to the 10.10 Glasgow to Birmingham on 21 July 1959, which it would work as far as Crewe. This was a regular Crewe North Pacific duty at this time. Notice the ample supply of coal on the tender!**
*Gavin Morrison*

Above:
**Another view of No 46235 *City of Birmingham*, but this is no bad thing, as this locomotive spent longer allocated to the North Shed than any other member of the class. Here it is, in nice external condition, at the head of the summer Saturdays 10.35 Glasgow to Euston, passing Low Gill in the awesome, but nonetheless beautiful Lune Gorge. What better place to portray what these locomotives were all about, than to show one in this, their home country, where they achieved their finest performances. The train set consists of the 'Caledonian' stock, suitably augmented, and not otherwise used on Saturdays.** *Gavin Morrison*

designed to elevate rail wagons so that their contents could be discharged directly into canal boats on the Cauldon Branch of The Trent & Mersey Canal. It was one of the first attempts to ease the burden of manual transhipment by pick and shovel and dated from 1917.

Doubtless, Coleman contributed some of the brainwork behind the achievements of J. A. Hookham, the last Locomotive Superintendent of the NSR and renowned as something of an innovator. Among other things he was responsible for the perfection of the cast iron piston rod packing, used by the LMS from its inception, by the other companies soon after, and eventually by steam engine builders all over the world. On amalgamation, Coleman moved to Horwich, and by 1933 was Chief Draughtsman there; Stanier soon moved him to Crewe, clearly spotted his talent, and in 1935 put him in sole charge of all production design, with headquarters at Derby. Thus it fell to Coleman to convert many of his Chief's ideas into practical designs, and his contribution to the finished locomotives should not be underestimated. In the magnificent 'Duchess' Pacifics, the perfect partnership of these two men reached its finale — I very nearly used the word fruition here, but there is little doubt that had

World War 2 not intervened, or had other circumstances demanded it, a further development of this design would have been equally successful, and even more impressive.

From their first introduction in 1937, Crewe North had 'Duchesses' on its allocation, and this remained the case until their final demise in October 1964, it being the last shed to which they were allocated. Generally, the North Shed engines — colloquially known to all and sundry there as 'Big Un's' — worked night trains northwards from Crewe on diagrams like the Euston to Glasgow, Perth and Aberdeen sleeping car, newspaper and mail trains. Some of these diagrams were the toughest footplate jobs ever regularly assigned in this country. From Crewe to Perth was 296 miles, and Crewe men worked right through with their engines between these two places, on a double-home basis. Perth men, it should be noted, never came to

Crewe, or south of Carlisle for that matter! The Perth link at Crewe North was the No 2 link, with eight sets of men in an eight-week cycle. These hardy souls worked three return trips to Perth during two of the eight weeks, two return trips during a further five weeks, and one trip each to Glasgow and London during the remaining week, out and home with the 'Midday Scot' in both cases. This last job was the only time the men saw daylight from the footplate during the winter months, and was in the link to ensure the men retained their route knowledge. Men either stayed in the link for years on end — because they loved it — or skipped it altogether because they hated it; therefore, it never really featured in the normal link progression at Crewe North.

There were many cases over the years where men went directly from fireman to driver in the Perth link, so unacceptable was it considered to be by many of them. To take but one example, George Preece started as a cleaner at Crewe North in 1923, passed for firing the following year, and went straight into the Perth link when he became a full fireman in 1936. He was to remain in it when he became a full driver in 1946, and did not leave it until he became one of the very first diesel instructors in 1957. A tremendous character George retired in 1970 and was typical of Crewe enginemen.

Incidentally, it is worthy of mention that George was the driver of the up 'Northern Irishman', working one of his rest days, on that fateful day of the appalling triple collision at Harrow on 8 October, 1952. George and his mate had booked on that morning with colleagues Driver R. S. (Bob) Jones and Fireman Colin Turnock, they were to re-man the up Perth, George and his mate the following Stranraer; the rest is history, and ironically the same Perth train north of Crewe was one of those George worked in his normal link. Both George and Bob Jones were working turns outside their normal links, and it was pure providence that each was not working the other's train that morning.

The through workings of engines and men between Crewe and Perth commenced in 1930, originally using 'Royal Scots'. The 'Tin Lizzies' (ie the 'Princess Royals') went on to the jobs almost from their inception, and the 'Big Uns' supplanted them almost totally, as soon as sufficient numbers were available. The men in the link would tend to share the same engine with another crew for quite long periods, and they would generally book on anything up to an hour before they were due off the shed because, despite the engines being prepared for them, that last drop of oil here and there, and that last minor adjustment was theirs, and theirs alone. The fireman would also pile on to the fire anything up to 2 tons of coal, and I have seen those massive fireboxes so full that the coal was almost touching the brick arch. It was normal practice at Crewe North to open the tender coal doors on the Pacifics by use of a coal hammer, and allow the contents to flood the footplate, all of which would then be shovelled on to the fire — 'filling the box' as it was called! Then, after closing the doors again, a trip was made under the coaling plant to top up the tender.

There was method in this apparent madness because Crewe, in view of its geographical position, got limited supplies of both Welsh and good Yorkshire coal, both considerably higher in terms of BTUs than the softer North Staffordshire and Lancashire grades otherwise supplied. They were, of course, and more importantly, vastly superior to the very soft Scottish stuff habitually on hand at Perth. Thus, not only would the fire generally last without any attention until Preston was reached, but there would be quite a bit left on arrival at Perth. If then the minimum was taken to fill the tender at the Scottish shed, by the time they were south of Carlisle on the way back, and the hard climbing was starting, the shovel would again be biting into the Welsh or Yorkshire hards! But stories are told of cutting things a little too fine, and if adverse circumstances were encountered, or delays or strong headwinds, pilots had to be taken south of Preston! Locomotives frequently arrived on the North Shed with their cupboards bare — how did they ever do it? I used to wonder.

This planned conservation of the fuel was one of the principal reasons why these locomotives were rarely used on fill-in turns during their daily sojourn at Perth, and much pressure was applied on the Scottish Region authorities to see that this was so; but it was a constant source of frustration to the enthusiast fraternity, seeing these two large engines slumbering on the shed all day.

The No 1 link at Crewe mainly covered the London and Carlisle jobs and the No 3 link the Glasgow jobs; like the Perth link this one also contained eight sets of men. Until the 70ft turntable was installed at Crewe North in 1950, the Pacifics had to be turned via the Gresty Lane-Sorting Sidings North triangle, or on very rare occasions on the 70ft table which had been installed at Crewe South in 1945. They were prohibited due to their length from using the North Staffordshire triangle between North Stafford Sidings, and Sorting Sidings North. However, the more general practice was to use the engines on fill-in diagrams to and from Shrewsbury. On arrival at Crewe on the up trains from Scotland the men would be relieved by a 'shed set', and they would take the engines on to the shed, dispose and then prepare them, before they were turned off again to work the West of England trains between Crewe and Shrewsbury. These included trains such as the Liverpool-Plymouth and the Manchester-Penzance, which left Crewe at mid-morning. On arrival at Shrewsbury the engine would be replaced by a Western Region one, and then proceed via the Severn Bridge triangle, to stable north of the station at Crewe Bank, and await the afternoon down West of England trains, which they would work to Crewe. On arrival back at Crewe they were of course the right way round to head north again after servicing that evening. These fill-in turns were nice easy footplate jobs, with several hours to spare at Shrewsbury.

But this is not what the Pacifics were all about. Most of their work was at night, and in my trainspotting days south of Crewe, at Whitmore or Madeley, I used to see between six to eight a day, on the up and down 'Royal Scot', 'Midday Scot' and later the 'Caledonian'; where were the other 32? The answer, I was later to discover, was resting between their night's exertions on Crewe North, Polmadie, and Perth Sheds, or other such places. This predominance of night workings was also the reason why, and what is perhaps not so well known, they were not all restored to the LMS maroon livery in the late 1950s. As this livery was more expensive to apply than the standard green, and as the diagrams were such that some sheds' engines worked night trains exclusively, whilst others similarly worked day trains, somebody decided it was pointless painting engines red at greater expense if nobody was going to see them. So those allocated to Crewe North and Polmadie, which sheds predominantly worked the night diagrams, tended to be left green, whilst those from Camden, Edge Hill and Carlisle, which tended to monopolise the daytime diagrams, were painted maroon. And so it was, although, of course, 'sod's law' being what it is, they often got mixed up, and once the diesels started to arrive, nobody bothered very much where individual locomotives were allocated in relation to diagrams anyway.

The Perth trains regularly loaded to 17 or 18 vehicles (570 tons tare or more) and although vehicles were often added and detached at Preston and Motherwell, generally the full tonnage had to be taken over the tougher sections including Shap and Beattock banks. Some of the real Crewe North stalwarts regularly worked these jobs, and the names of Bill Rawlins, Charlie Jones and Arthur Smith are recalled as drivers in the late 1930s and early 1940s; later, along with George Preece, Jack Blackburn, Harry Speed, Albert Marks, Bill Lounds, Jimmy Woodvine and George (Bud) Ollier were drivers in the link, each of whom had fired to their predecessors. 'Bud' is recalled as about the only man who would relish the prospect of taking the Standard BR Class 8 Pacific No 71000 on a trip to Perth, and hence, her visits to that city were rare!

Originally, and until about 1952, there were no barracks at Perth for enginemen, and the men lodged in private accommodation found for them — usually the homes of other railwaymen — and they tended to go back to the same place time and time again. Amazing tales are told of the Perth trains, and it is difficult for me to pay them proper justice here and a few stories must suffice. One can read of hundreds of very creditable efforts by these locomotives in the writings of O. S. Nock, C. J. Allen and others, but of the real work during the night hours, one can read little or nothing. Actually, the trains themselves were not all that tightly timed point-to-point, but there were many and frequent stops, with station time being consistently exceeded as mails and newspapers were loaded or unloaded and connections awaited. To achieve on-time arrivals therefore, high power outputs and speeds were needed, not revealed by the timetables, and banking engines were rarely taken over either Shap or Beattock banks: this was just not

done! Indeed, even with 18 vehicles it was considered a slight if a banker was taken. Grayrigg was the tester, and provided they could breast that bank without too much trouble, it would be 'right away' Glasgow! It was generally reckoned that after breasting Shap on the return journey it would not be necessary to touch either the regulator or the brake before attacking the slight rise between Lancaster station and Lancaster No 1 signalbox. Anybody who has a knowledge of this road will realise the significance of this. (Anybody who has not, need only glance at the gradient profile!) The mind can only boggle at the speeds reached around the curves at Low Gill — eased considerably, I hasten to add, over the years since the diesels and electrics arrived. 'Kid, I have seen sparks coming off the buffer beam when passing the platform at Low Gill . . .' But these magnificent locomotives would ride like the proverbial Rolls-Royce under any circumstances and the men, working with them day in and day out (or should it be night in and night out?) knew exactly what they could and could not do. I once asked George what sort of speeds they achieved after speedometers were fitted. 'Kid', he said, 'they frightened the lives out of us and we were repeatedly booked for losing time!'

In reliability terms, in George's years in the link, he could never recall coming back from Perth with a different engine than they had gone North with, neither can he remember having to change engines en route. What more can one say? They were real enginemen's engines if ever such existed, and the only limitation on their ability to shift heavy tonnage was the ability of the men to put coal through the door. And any footplateman will warm to an engine with these characteristics, whose prowess was strictly related to theirs, and whose upper limit they were never able to reach. I mentioned earlier how it was the practice to 'fill the box' before leaving on the Perth jobs — the Glasgow trips were no different — and one might assume that this would have had a choking effect. But the men knew that they would never be able to exert the locomotive or get anywhere near its upper limits on the generally easy road to Preston, with its heavy traffic density, numerous speed restrictions for mining subsidence and the like. They would be well on towards Milnthorpe before

they really needed to start opening the engine out, as the Fells approached and the nine miles from Oxenholme to Grayrigg at grades averaging around 1 in 110 came upon them. But by this time the fire would be nicely burnt through, and firing a 'Big Un' was comparatively easy, and provided one could get the coal through the door and in the back corners, and in the quantity needed, the engine would do the rest. They were magnificent steaming locomotives and, when in good nick, with a fire of the right size, would tackle the Westmorland hills — 17 or 18 behind them — against both injectors, and with a whiff of steam at their safety valves; but to achieve this, both driver and fireman had to get their shirts wet! They very often did. Bankers, who wants b . . . bankers with engines like this?

Enginemen always value good steaming locomotives, and they will forgive almost any other ailment in a steam locomotive provided it will steam — rough riding, hard riding, uncomfortable, draughty, you name it, but they will run away from a bad steamer. Imagine then, a locomotive fully master of all pitted against it, a beautiful rider to boot, and hardly a thing to complain about — Utopia. I have written elsewhere about the reception given by Crewe North men to the BR Standard Class 8 Pacific No 71000, and illustrated why this locomotive — in my opinion — would never have made the grade with Crewe men, even if it had steamed better. These men had had successive improvements in power on their northern jobs, and many of them would recall firing LNWR 'Princes', 'Claughtons', and later LMS 'Royal Scots', each a distinct improvement on what had gone before. To beat a 'Big Un', therefore, No 71000 not only had to equal the LMS engine in all respects, but it had to surpass it in at least one sphere. Thus, as a shy steamer, it never had a chance, and as a result made but a few trips to Perth, and not an enormous number north of Crewe, especially in its later years. Significantly, its withdrawal predated all the 'Big Uns', and I recall its arrival on Crewe North after its last main line run; nobody shed any tears.

During the latter days of private ownership, the LMS in an attempt to improve the availability, and the reliability, of the locomotives, as well as the smaller 'Tin Lizzies', decided to concentrate all the larger valve and piston examinations on the Pacifics at

80

# 6
# NSR and GWR Intrusions

We have already seen how the small but nonetheless formidable NSR was the only pre-grouping railway company to penetrate by a direct line the LNWR stronghold of Crewe. Therefore it justly deserves to be dealt with first in this chapter, which also chronicles the history of the GWR's locomotive shed activity at Crewe.

The NSR line between Stoke-on-Trent and Crewe opened to both passenger and goods traffic on 9 October 1848, and this section was a part of the NSR's original system. The remaining sections were from Colwich and Norton Bridge (both of which were junctions with the LNWR, one north and one south of Stafford) to Stoke, and on to Kidsgrove, junction with the lines to Crewe and Macclesfield where connection was again made with the LNWR system, this time onwards to Manchester. There was also a continuation south-eastward from Stoke to Burton-on-Trent, and later on a branch from Stoke to Derby.

Very little is known about the NSR shed at Crewe, except that it was a single-road affair 100ft long, and situated on the down side of the NSR line as it entered Crewe in the apex formed by the line to Stoke and the main LNWR line south. It opened in late 1871, cost but £460, and was alongside Crewe North Stafford Sidings signalbox. The remains of a pit and other facilities existed thereabouts until quite recently, undoubtedly remnants of the erstwhile shed building. This shed would have had a capacity for around three locomotives, which is about the number that always seems to have been its allocation, and they would have principally been used on the Crewe-Stoke-Derby and Burton-on-Trent passenger workings. The NSR goods and mineral locomotives would have tended to be diagrammed on an out and home basis from Stoke and later Alsager too, and would not normally have had to lay over at Crewe, though doubtless they

did visit the shed from time to time. However, prior to the opening of Alsager Shed in 1890, it is known that one of the Audley line shunting and trip engines came from Crewe Shed; this branch had opened in 1870.

Below:
**Almost indistinguishable in this photograph is the only known view of the North Stafford Shed at Crewe, seen here on the extreme left, along with the North Stafford Sidings signalbox. The train approaching from the south is hauled by an 'Alfred the Great' four-cylinder compound, and one of the three-cylinder compound 0-8-0 goods engines can be seen on the right. Notice the difference in the elegant McKenzie & Holland North Stafford signals to the left, and the standard LNWR pattern elsewhere. The photograph, which is from a LNWR revised series of postcards dated November 1904, would have been taken some years before then. The Carriage Shed later occupied the site immediately behind the train.**
*Collection Dr J. R. Hollick*

SCOTCH EXPRESS APPROACHING CREWE.

Above:
**An immaculate Fowler Class 4 2-6-4T No 42315, allocated to Stoke Shed, but not as long-serving a member of that shed's fleet as many other members of the class were, and seen here about to depart from Platform 6B on 22 March 1960. As this was after the introduction of DMUs on most of the local workings, the train would probably be the unadvertised 16.26 Crewe to Cresswell staff train for the Radway Green ROF factory workers; this train ran as Empty Coaching Stock (ECS) between Crewe and Radway Green, both morning and evening.** A. Swain

The shed was an early casualty following grouping, and is recorded as having closed its doors for the last time on 30 March 1923, with the locomotives and men going to Crewe North. It is interesting at this point to mention that closure was some four months before the NSR officially became a constituent of the LMS for, despite the LMS being formed on 1 January 1923, the NSR and the Caledonian Railway, due to some legal complication, did not amalgamate until 1 July. However, to all intents and purposes, from an operational aspect, the NSR had been part of the new group from 1 January, along with all the other constituents and absorbed companies.

It is perhaps surprising that the NSR maintained its own establishment at Crewe for so long because, admittedly after problems in the early years, it was on excellent relations with its larger neighbour. Indeed, the NSR housed its engines and men — on a regular diagrammed basis — in the LNWR sheds at Longsight (Manchester), Edge Hill (Liverpool) and Stafford, and one is left wondering why it did not come to a similar arrangement at Crewe, and thus save the expense of a separate establishment.

Although the NSR was very much a tank engine railway, Crewe's allocation over the years seems to have consisted of at least one of the several NSR 2-4-0 tender engine classes. These predominated on the Crewe to Derby and Burton-on-Trent passenger workings, which were amongst the longest runs regularly operated by the NSR. There would usually be a tank engine too, for shunting and local trip workings; latterly this would be one of the numerous and very popular 'D' Class 0-6-0Ts. After the demise of the 2-4-0s, one of the company's few 4-4-0 tender engines, No 170, built at Stoke in 1910, was stationed at Crewe to work the first train to Derby and Burton each morning. After closure of the shed, demolition seems to have been swift, but locomotive watering facilities existed at Crewe North Stafford Sidings until the end of steam, and it would seem that these were left after the shed closed, and

adapted to serve locomotives standing in the down loop, which was alongside the signalbox.

The GWR reached Crewe by virtue of its running powers from Nantwich-Market Drayton Junction, where its line from Wellington joined the LNWR line from Crewe to Shrewsbury. The 10¾-mile section from Nantwich to Market Drayton opened on 19 October 1863, originally as an independent company, but operated by the GWR from inception. There appears to have been a locomotive shed at Market Drayton almost from

opening, and the line was operated from that end. In October 1867 the line was extended from Market Drayton to Wellington, making it 26½ miles long in all, and the shed at Market Drayton seems to have been sold to the NSR, when the latter railway arrived at the Shropshire market town with the opening of its line from Silverdale on 1 February 1870.

Presumably as a result of the GWR line opening through to Wellington, locomotives needed to be serviced at Crewe, rather than working out and home from Market Drayton, where they had been serviced before. Incidentally, the GWR had running powers between Nantwich and Crewe over the LNWR granted as a part of the Act of Incorporation of the Nantwich & Market Drayton Railway. Indeed, the Act made provision for quite elaborate working arrangements, and for the first few years the LNWR seems to have actually worked the Nantwich & Market Drayton traffic on behalf of the GWR. It would appear that as a prerequisite of the LNWR (and other companies too) withdrawing its opposition to the GWR and West Midland Railway Amalgamation Bill (Vic 25-26 Ch v; Royal Assent 13 July 1863), clauses were inserted in the Act, providing mutually agreed facilities, regarding all matters of issue between the two companies — and there were many! Presumably, as a result of this the LNWR agreed to work on the GWR's behalf the Nantwich & Market Drayton Railway, and may indeed have continued to do so until the former company's system became connected to Market Drayton with the opening of the line from Wellington in 1867. The Crewe Shed was located alongside the Shrewsbury line west of Crewe itself, and on the down side

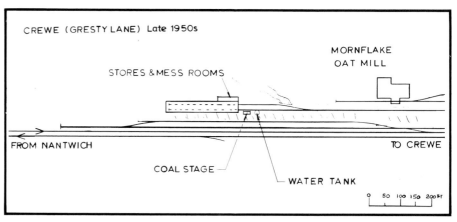

CREWE (GRESTY LANE) Late 1950s

MORNFLAKE OAT MILL

STORES & MESS ROOMS

FROM NANTWICH

TO CREWE

COAL STAGE

WATER TANK

0    50   100  150  200 Ft

*Below:*
**Another view of Gresty Lane, this time taken on 25 March 1962, and again showing one of the Wellington-allocated Ivatt tanks, this time No 41232, and showing the tenders of two Western Region 4-6-0s protruding from the shed. Whilst the tank engines worked the passenger jobs over the Market Drayton branch bunker-first on the way home, tender engines would be turned on the Gresty Lane triangle on arrival at Crewe, before going to the shed for servicing; hence unfortunately most views of them on shed show them this way round.** *J. K. Williams*

at a much lower level to the main line. It was almost opposite the later site of the wagon shop yard, west of the Gresty Lane bridge, and near to the eventual site of the Mornflake Oat Mill which still stands today. Gresty Lane No 1 signalbox controlled entry to the shed yard, as well as controlling the triangular junction with the Independent goods lines, and access to the wagon shop and transhipment shed.

Originally, the shed seems to have had capacity for around four locomotives on two roads, but it was extended by 1910 to a final dimension of 220ft by 35ft, with two full length block-end roads, and with room for around double the original number of locomotives. Brick-built, to the then

standard LNWR hip roof pattern, there was a small hand coaling stage and water tower at the entrance to the shed, between the building itself and the main line. As with most sheds, sundry other small outbuildings existed and the offices, stores and mess rooms, etc, were housed in a lean-to building on the northern wall of the shed. Seemingly, although owned by the GWR, this shed was built by the LNWR on behalf of the GWR, and on land leased to it; this perhaps was another example of the co-operation generated by the 1863 GWR-West Midland Railway Amalgamation Act.

Over the years the allocation seems to have hovered in the region of three to eight locomotives, and at

Nationalisation consisted of 2-6-2Ts Nos 4154 and 5139, with 0-6-0PT No 3749. Gresty Lane, as the shed was known, was always a sub-shed of Wellington, itself part of the Wolverhampton Stafford Road Area, which was coded WLN in GWR days, and 84H by BR; Stafford Road Shed itself carrying the code 84A. The main work performed by the locomotives was the Crewe to Wellington passenger service turns with some freight via the same route, and prior to the formation of British Railways in January 1948 this branch and the former Cambrian route from Whitchurch to Oswestry provided the only normal routes for GWR locomotives into Crewe. But the Oswestry workings only dated from during World War 2, and even then the practice of changing the engines off the Cambrian section with LMR ones at Whitchurch returned, and generally remained except for the odd working, until Whitchurch Shed closed in September 1957. As well as LMR men, the Western Region had a set of men at Whitchurch too. However,

after Nationalisation, Western Region locomotive workings into Crewe direct from Shrewsbury, rather than Wellington or Oswestry, occurred occasionally, and this would generally bring the bigger express passenger types, which would usually visit either the North or South Sheds for servicing and, of course, turning. There were never any locomotive turning facilities at Gresty Lane, and any locomotives visiting that shed needing turning had to go to one or other of the LNWR sheds, or more usually turn via the triangle between Gresty Lane No 1, Salop Goods Junction and Basford Hall Sorting Sidings North.

When the Crewe to Manchester and Liverpool lines were electrified, the former from 9 September 1960, and the latter from 1 January 1962, the practice of changing Western Region for LMR motive power on the North-West to the West of England passenger trains at Shrewsbury ceased. Clearly, this would have been uneconomic when locomotives had to be changed again, for electric power, 33 miles further on at Crewe. Henceforth, the Western Region locomotives were diagrammed through to Crewe, by this date all being rostered for 'Warship' or the later 'Western' type diesel hydraulic

classes, which were fuelled and serviced at Crewe North prior to their return workings. However, if as sometimes happened, the diagrammed diesel locomotive had been substituted by a steam engine, then it too worked through to Crewe, and it was only after this fundamental change in locomotive diagramming that the larger Western Region passenger classes, the 'Castles' and 'Halls', could be seen with any regularity at Crewe. Like the diesels, they would go to the North Shed for servicing, and I recall my very first sighting of the famous No 4079 *Pendennis Castle*, one member of the class that had always seemed to elude me previously, on Crewe North one morning during the summer of 1962. Later of course, as steam locomotives became more and more run-down, and sections of the Western Region were transferred to the LMR, visits of the larger Western Region engines to Crewe on freight trains became quite common.

Gresty Lane depot survived, surprisingly on the nationalised railway, and still as an outpost of Wellington providing power for the Market Drayton branch, until closure came on 17 June 1963. Latterly, the branch power consisted of former LMS Ivatt Class 2 2-6-2Ts. It was amazing that

*Below:*
**Ivatt tank No 41232 again, this time about to depart from Platform 3B with the 16.20 train to Wellington, on 23 September 1961.** *Michael Mensing*

Above:
**Another view of a train standing at Platform 3B, the 'Western bay' as it was known, and showing 'Manor' class 4-6-0 No 7809 *Childrey Manor*, about to depart with the 19.45 to Oswestry 89A, where the locomotive was allocated at this time. This was the return working of a regular 'Manor' diagram that brought the engine to Crewe with a train from Aberystwyth in the late afternoon.** *Michael Mensing*

Above right:
**No 7809 *Childrey Manor* again, leaving Crewe with the same train as in the previous view, but on 29 June 1959. There were few places where Western Region locomotives could be seen working 'under the wires', and Crewe was one.** *R. O. Tuck*

Right:
**By the time this photograph was taken on 5 May 1963, the roof of Gresty Lane Shed had either collapsed, or been removed for safety reasons, and the shed only had a few more months life. Seen here is 'Manor' class 4-6-0 No 7824 *Ilford Manor*, belonging to Wolverhampton Oxley Depot; it would have arrived on a freight from the Wellington direction and, unusually, had not been turned ready for its return journey, before arrival on the shed. It is in rather grimy condition, in complete contrast to the engines of the same class that worked into Crewe from the Cambrian system, and which were always immaculate. Also on the shed this day were; 'Grange' class 4-6-0s Nos 6812/26/45 and 50, and 0-6-0PT No 3744. The latter would have worked the 'Passenger' from Wellington, vice the, by this date, normal Ivatt Class 2.** *Mike Fell*

nobody had got around to closing it earlier, and when the end came it was because of the boundary changes that had taken place between Western and London Midland Regions from 1 January that year, and for no other reason. Doubtless, however, before much longer somebody would have done something! On 1 January 1963, large sections of the Western Region in Mid-Wales, the border counties and south Staffordshire passed to LMR control, and this included the Wolverhampton Stafford Road Motive Power Area, and thus Wellington, and with it the workings that Crewe Gresty Lane served. Thus by a quirk of railway organisation, this little outpost of the erstwhile GWR survived amidst the enormous LMS empire at Crewe tucked away, almost out of sight, and certainly out of mind! However, some interchange of crews did take place, and the Western Region crews were controlled as necessary by the LMR Crewe Control office, thus giving better utilisation in many cases. Indeed, with its crews it seems to have officially passed to LMR control

when it was recorded as becoming a sub-shed of Crewe North from 19 April 1953. There was an extensive change-round of Regional locomotive stocks on this date and, for example, former LMS locomotives at Swansea became Western Region stock, and the 68 ex-LNER 06 Class (ie LMS type '8F' 2-8-0s, built during World War 2 for the LNER) allocated to the Eastern, North Eastern and Scottish Regions, were transferred to become LMR stock. However, as we have already seen, little changed and to all intents and purposes Gresty Lane remained a Western Region depot. The Crewe to Wellington and Oswestry workings remained the responsibility of the Western Region, with their own locomotives, and the Wellington engines continued to be serviced and repaired at Gresty Lane between trips. It was rare for the Oswestry locomotives or any others off the Cambrian system to visit any of the Crewe sheds, as after turning they normally worked home again almost immediately. Gresty Lane seems to have had few visitors over the years, if the number of photographs which seem to be available are anything to go by, but it provided one of those extremely interesting small backwaters of railway history and operation.

The locomotives and men on closure were transferred to either the North or South Sheds, but the principal reason for the shed's long survival did not outlast it very long, and the passenger service between

Crewe and Wellington ceased on and from 9 September 1962. The branch lingered on for freight traffic until final closure came on 1 May 1967. It did serve as a useful diversionary route, and for a time the 'Pines Express' regularly went by this route. The shed was demolished soon after closure, but parts of its site could still be seen for a long time afterwards, along with the remains of the filled-in inspection pits.

Left:
The Western Region 'Warship' diesel-hydraulic locomotives were regular visitors to Crewe in the early 1960s, until the Class 47s arrived on the scene. Here can be seen No D829 *Magpie*, at the south end of the down through road, proceeding from the North Shed to await the arrival of a train bound for the West of England, which it would take over for its onward journey; 11 April 1964. *N. Clarke*

Centre left:
The Southern Region Class 33 1,550hp Type 3 diesel locomotives commenced working some extremely complicated cyclic diagrams based on their home depot of Eastleigh, from the early 1980s, and these included the Cardiff to Crewe workings. Here can be seen No 33008, named after its home depot, approaching Crewe South Junction, past Gresty Lane No 2 signalbox on 6 October 1984, with a train from Cardiff. To the right can be seen the Mornflake Oat Mill, and the Western Region shed was situated between the main line and the mill. At the time of writing these Cardiff trains are worked by Class 37/4 locomotives.
*Gavin Morrison*

Below:
On the same day as the previous view, No 33008 can be seen leaving Crewe with the 16.02 to Cardiff. To the right can be seen the connection to the Independent freight avoiding lines and Basford Hall Marshalling Yard, and to the extreme left part of the Mornflake Oat Mill. Notice the locomotive is fitted with miniature snow ploughs. Amazing multi-regional utilisation was achieved by these locomotives during the period 1980-86, after years of being confined to the Southern Region. *Gavin Morrison*

# 7
# Diesel Depot

We saw in an earlier chapter how, as a part of the large reorganisation and modernisation of the Crewe motive power scene, it was proposed that a completely new depot be built, south of the station on the down side between the station itself and the South Junction. This new depot, intended from inception to be a 'concentration' repair depot (officially described as 'Examination & Repair Shop') was designed within the overall strategy of segregating the mileage and larger periodical examinations, along with wheeldrop work and heavy repairs, away from the inherently far dirtier servicing facilities. The reasoning behind this was twofold: first, by concentrating this type of work where the locomotives need not be in steam, much better working conditions and thus standards could be obtained; it was by this time already becoming increasingly difficult to recruit young men into skilled trades in the conditions appertaining to the average locomotive running shed. Secondly, it would allow such work to be concentrated in one depot, covering the allocated fleets of locomotives from not only all the depots in the Crewe Motive Power area, but other adjacent areas too. We have already seen how all the LMR-based Pacifics were given their larger mileage examination at Crewe North anyway.

Thus the running sheds themselves would be able to concentrate on the smaller X day examinations, minor repairs, washouts, etc, along with the day-by-day servicing; locomotives in steam would not be allowed in the new depot. The cynics would say that this philosophy was the same as that of the former LMS outstation repair depots, like Rugby, Polmadie and Perth for example, and which ironically had then only recently been phased out. But they were far larger establishments, far better equipped, and capable of undertaking work akin to a main workshop like Crewe or Derby. This new concentration depot, whilst capable of perhaps undertaking a slightly higher level of repair than had traditionally been undertaken in running sheds was, by and large, only intended to undertake the same sort of work.

The site chosen, on the down side of the main line, was between the Old Yard (sometimes referred to as the Down Yard) and the cutting which took the Independent lines from Basford Hall marshalling yards, to Salop Goods Junction, and onwards to the north. It was between the southern end of the station platforms and the junction of the line to Shrewsbury. Prior to the construction of the depot, an extremely large mound of earth, mainly clay, had to be removed, and this had been

deposited there many years before when the cutting was dug. Known as the 'Big Dig', the work had been undertaken in the period 1896-1901, and along with the associated Independent lines and burrowing tunnels, had kept well over 1,000 men employed; it cost around £500,000. The earth removed for the new depot was loaded into railway wagons and taken to the railway tip at Betley Road, south of Crewe on the main line towards Stafford; this work commenced in 1955, the drawings being dated June 1954 and recorded as having been received by the local civil engineer in March 1955.

Below:
**Early diesel activity at Crewe. Seen here are the pioneer main line diesel locomotives built for use in Britain, English Electric/Derby built Co-Cos Nos 10000 and 10001, approaching from the north, and having just passed under Earle Street Bridge. Notice that both locomotives are still in their original livery of black with aluminium relief, No 10000 still having its LMS insignia; they were repainted in the then standard green in 1956. Although always allocated to Willesden, these locomotives had their heavier maintenance undertaken at Crewe, once the Diesel Depot was open. At the period of this photograph, it was usual to use the locomotives as a pair on the Anglo-Scottish workings, and they would appear to be on a train from Glasgow in this view dating from c1949-50.** *Collection Harry Newbiggin*

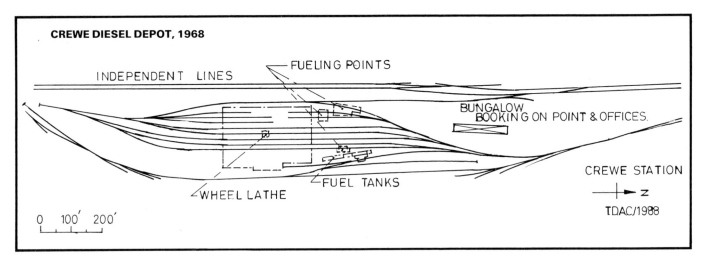

**CREWE DIESEL DEPOT, 1968**

INDEPENDENT LINES

FUELING POINTS

BUNGALOW
BOOKING ON POINT & OFFICES.

WHEEL LATHE

FUEL TANKS

CREWE STATION

TDAC/1988

0    100'    200'

Right from the scheme's commencement, it was intended to provide space within the depot for the diesel shunting locomotives allocated at Crewe South, and then being maintained within that steam depot, with all the disadvantages this gave. There were limited facilities for the few main line diesels then running, namely the ex-LMS twins Nos 10000 and 10001, and the former Southern Region trio, Nos 10201, 10202, and 10203. However, long before the building was complete, the 1955 Modernisation Plan was published, and this proclaimed the gradual replacement of steam traction in favour of diesel and electric; therefore, a decision was made to use the new depot, on completion, for maintenance of the new diesel locomotives and multiple-

units in its entirety, and various modifications were made in the latter stages of construction to meet this end. For example, the projected electric wheeldrop was never installed, and instead, an underground Atlas wheel-turning machine was fitted into the space originally intended for it. This machine, not scrapped until autumn 1987, was capable of turning locomotive and other rolling stock tyres, whilst the wheels themselves remained under the vehicle. Actually, it was more akin to a milling machine than a lathe, and used a milling hob, shaped to the profile of the tyre being turned, and containing many small individual milling cutters. However, the axle was held between centres, and of all BR's first generation wheel-turning

machines the Atlas was undoubtedly the best. Alternative machines were generally centreless wheel-profiling lathes, and these were slow, and very often less accurate. Significantly, of all the first generation machines, only the Atlas has any sort of future, and

Below:
**The other early main line diesels were the Southern Railway-inspired trio, Nos 10201-3, designed by Bulleid with English Electric, and all used on the LMR from early in their life. Here is No 10201, a 1,750hp 1Co-Co1, leaving No 3 platform at Crewe with a train for Euston on 21 July 1962. This was towards the end of the locomotives' working life, but the trio were the prototypes for the Class 40s, and their bogie arrangement was also perpetuated on Classes 44, 45 and 46.**
*The late Brian Haresnape*

such machines remain in use at Cricklewood (London), Shields (Glasgow), Doncaster, Laira (Plymouth) and Stratford (London). The installation of lathes capable of *in situ* tyre turning became so necessary with the spread of the newer types of traction, where not only were much smaller wheels used than on steam locomotives, but much more mileage per locomotive was accrued with the greater utilisation possible. Thus, unlike steam locomotives, which could generally be relied upon to go between works overhauls before tyre reprofiling became necessary, the diesels and electrics would need several visits to a lathe to restore the tyre profiles in between; so something quicker than having to take wheels out of the locomotive was clearly essential. Indeed, it is not

unknown for some of the higher mileage locomotives, or locomotives used on lines with a lot of sharp curvature, like the West Highland, to need new tyres between the periodicity of workshop overhauls. This is especially so with the extended timescales being developed under the BRB's new Maintenance Policy.

Despite this, the depot did finish up with a lot of equipment and facilities that were little or never used. For example, coppersmiths', whitemetalling and blacksmiths' shops were not the necessity that they had been in steam depots, neither was such a level of machine tools as had been provided. The depot was equipped with a full range, including a 12in gap lathe large enough to swing an axlebox, and a 24in shaper with sufficient stroke to machine a crosshead. Only at the eleventh hour was the order for an axle journal lathe cancelled. Other machines included a radial arm drill, 9½in centre lathe and rough and smooth grinders. The final drawing detailing the 'Alterations for Diesels' was dated June 1958 and included the wheel lathe installation details.

As completed the building contained five 270ft-long through roads, numbered 1-5 from the main line, with No 4 road having the Atlas lathe at its mid-point. At the south end there were three shorter roads, 80ft long and known as 6, 7 and 8 roads

south; all were traversed by a 2½-ton electric overhead travelling crane. There were two similar short roads at the north end, Nos 6 and 7 north, likewise traversed by an overhead crane, but in this case its longitudinal movement was by hand chain from ground level. The space between the two roads was occupied by a large brick-built sole-bar height platform, and as this bay was intended for the maintenance of diesel shunting locomotives, this platform was to give better access to their engine rooms when the side doors were open.

The space between the two sets of bay roads was occupied by the previously mentioned workshops, machine tools and electrical substation. The staff amenities, consisting of locker and mess rooms, toilets and washing facilities, together with offices and stores, were along the eastern wall of the depot; there were such facilities for a total of 100 staff, with 80 being on duty at any one time.

Other facilities provided consisted of a 14,000gal fuelling installation, at the north end of the depot and alongside No 1 road, lubricating oil dispersing points at the south end of all roads within the shed, fixed battery chargers and compressed air supplies throughout the building. The depot was 280ft long and 141ft wide with three hipped roofs, the two outer ones each covering three roads, and

Below:
**A November 1957 view inside the new Diesel Depot, showing Nos 6 and 7 bay roads at the north end, which were specially designed for the maintenance of diesel shunting locomotives — hence the elevated platform between them. Notice the 2½-ton overhead travelling crane. The two fitters have just removed a cylinder head from the locomotive, and on the right is Fred Bayman, one of the best known of the supervisors at the depot until his retirement a few years ago. On the extreme left can be seen another fitter, Bob Capewell, testing a fuel injector; Bob is currently in charge of Chester Diesel Depot.**
*British Railways No DM2169*

the middle one two roads. Rail access was from the northern end, with all eight roads at the southern end converging into a single head shunt; there was, however, a run-round road to the eastern side of the depot, and between it and the Independent line cutting. Additionally, there was an emergency connection between No 1 road, to the north end of the depot, and the Old Yard. To the east of the main building, the offices, stores and amenity block occupied the full length of the shed, being 27ft wide — 33ft wide in the area of the stores.

Diesel multiple-units (DMUs) had started to operate in the Crewe area prior to the opening of the new depot in late 1957, particularly to and from Stoke-on-Trent and Derby. Purpose-built facilities for their maintenance were constructed at Derby Etches Park, and Stoke Cockshute Sidings; however, at Crewe modifications were undertaken at the Carriage shed. This large building was on the up side of the main line, south of the South Junction, and on the opposite side of the main line to the South Shed; it was an old building dating from the turn of the century. One of the roads, that on the eastern side, had its very shallow pit reconstructed

and deepened, and a fuelling installation was built south of the building. Thereafter, the smaller examinations and servicing of the new units was undertaken there, with the sets going over to the new depot for the larger examinations and heavy repairs, like engine, gearbox and final drive renewals. For a time, Crewe had its own allocation of DMUs, but with the increase in the number of main line diesels to be maintained, from 1964 the allocation was transferred to Derby, Stoke and Chester. Henceforth, only minor repairs and servicing were undertaken at Crewe Carriage Shed, but many sets were fuelled and stabled there overnight, and between diagrams.

We saw earlier how facilities for the smaller examinations, repairs and fuelling of the diesel locomotives had been installed at Crewe North; similar facilities, dating from before World War 2 existed at Crewe South too, and shunting locomotives continued to be stabled and fuelled there. Hence, the new depot was not originally called upon to perform these functions, only the bigger examinations, and repairs. Originally, like steam locomotives, the diesel examinations were undertaken on a

mileage basis, starting at a 5,000-6,000-mile interval, with a larger examination at 20,000-24,000 miles and so on. Later, about 1964, this was changed to a system based on the actual hours the diesel engine had been running, this being more compatible with the work the mechanical parts of the locomotive had done. Obviously, the number of hours the engine had been running and, therefore, the wear and tear it had suffered, did not correlate with the miles the locomotive had run. This system, with several alterations, in the main relating to how the actual hours are calculated, has remained in use to this day.

Not only were the Crewe-allocated diesel main line locomotives maintained and repaired at the new depot (which became known as Crewe Diesel Depot) but those from the other West Coast main line sheds too. Thus the English Electric Type 4s (later Class 40) — then the principal motive power for the West Coast main line passenger services — all came to Crewe for such work. Locomotives from Camden, Longsight, Edge Hill and Carlisle Upperby, all came to Crewe, along with a smattering from other depots and of

Above left:
**Another view inside the new depot, taken at the same time as the previous one, and showing the three-bay roads at the southern end, and the machine shop area. Notice in the centre the wooden fencing around the pit where the wheel lathe was to be installed, this was the site originally intended for the wheel-drop. In front of it are parts of the overhead travelling crane ready to be installed over the southern bay roads. The shallow pit in front of the machine tools was intended for the axle journal turning lathe: the view looks north.**
*British Railways No DM2165*

Above:
**Another November 1957 view, this time illustrating the northern end of the machine shop. Behind the driver standing in front of the main line diesel, No 10001, can just be discerned a hydraulic press. Intended for pressing bushes out of motion parts, this was later transferred to Crewe South.**
*British Railways No DM2167*

Right:
**An unusual view of the down 'Red Rose' stopped by signals alongside the Carriage Shed, and just south of Crewe South Junction. It was in this shed that much of the servicing work was done on the Crewe-allocated diesel railcar sets. The engine is Rebuilt 'Patriot' No 45521 *Rhyl*, allocated to Edge Hill and working home, the photograph being taken from the footbridge which connected the South Shed and Carriage Shed Yards.**
*The late Eric Treacy*

other types. Crewe North had a small allocation of 'Baby-Sulzer' Type 2s (later Class 24-5), and the occasional English Electric Type 1 (later Class 20) also found its way to the Diesel Depot. Additionally, any locomotive turned off Crewe Works, either after a classified or unclassified repair, came to the depot for a daily (later A) exam, and to be commissioned so to speak; in this way many other types made short visits over the years as the workshops got involved in repairing different types.

Prior to the closure of Crewe North in October 1965, a scheme was developed to take over the smaller examinations and servicing undertaken there. This involved dedicating No 1 road as a 'running road', for want of a better term, where locomotives could have A examinations (the erstwhile daily exam, by this time undertaken at a 23-32hr interval), and running repairs undertaken as they proceeded through the depot, and before being stabled ready for their next turn of duty. The fuelling installations had to be upgraded, and their capacity increased, with an additional point being installed between Nos 1 and 2 roads,

alongside the existing one. A much smaller installation intended for the shunting locomotives and situated between Nos 6 and 7 roads at the northern end was enlarged at the same time, so that locomotives could be fuelled, if necesary, whilst standing on the run-round road. Storage capacity had to be increased too, and this was achieved by moving two of the fixed tank installations from the North Shed, and installing them alongside the existing ones at the Diesel Depot, the other two being similarly removed after the North Shed had finally ceased to service the diesels.

An important part of the plan was an additional access road to the depot, and this was provided by building a new section of railway to connect the run-round road at the western side of the shed, at its northern end, to the up Independent line between Salop Goods Junction and Crewe North Junction; a cross-over road was installed simultaneously between the up and down Independents at the point of junction. The system was that locomotives would enter the depot as before, and this route would henceforth become

Above:
**English Electric Type 4 diesels Nos 233 *Empress of England*, and 216 *Campania*, standing outside the north end of the Diesel Depot early on the morning of 30 June 1969. This was after preparation, and prior to them working light to Willesden, then to work the Royal Train to Caernarvon, on the occasion of the Investiture of the Prince of Wales. From left to right can be seen: the Author, Fitters Dick Roberts, Barry Harding, George Browness, Dave Morgan, Tony Hope and George Barber. Fitter's Mates 'Dan' Archer and Charlie Skelling, Fitter Fred Roberts, Fitter's Mate Ted Owen, Fitters Ossie Jones and Les Surridge, Fitter's Mate Bob Dutton and Electrician Alec Watt; on the steps of No 233 can be seen an Electrician.**
*Allan Baker*

the inlet. They would proceed to the fuelling points each side of No 1 road, then enter No 1 road of the shed for servicing, A examinations and running repairs, etc, before leaving the depot via the run-round line and the new connection — which would become the outlet. Of course, each connection was multi-directional, so the system could be reversed if either road was blocked for any reason. Likewise, locomotives could be fuelled on No 2 road, or as they left the depot by use of the extended facilities on No 7 road south.

Many problems were encountered in the construction of the new connection to the Independent lines. Remember that much of the ground hereabouts was made up of clay removed during construction of the Independent line cuttings and there was much subsidence. Problems continued after opening, and a lot of work had to be undertaken on the cutting sides to retain the slipping clay.

For some years after closure of the North Shed a small fan of sidings there was retained for locomotive stabling, and these sidings became known as Crewe North Holding Sidings. Room to stable locomotives at the Diesel Depot was severely limited, and it became the practice to ferry them in twos and threes between Diesel Depot and North Holding Sidings after attention. They would be 'stacked up' on the run-round road, until there were sufficient to make a ferry run viable. There were, of course, occasions when locomotives went directly off the Diesel Depot to take up diagrams.

As the use of steam traction declined, and the numbers of diesels increased, the number of staff at the Diesel Depot rose; many men transferred from the North and South Sheds, together with others recruited from outside industries. Some transferred from the main workshops, and nearby sheds like Stoke and Northwich when they closed. Of course, most craftsmen at Crewe, wherever they worked — Rolls-Royce being the other large engineering employer — had been railway-trained, so the amount of retraining needed was small. To cater for these staff increases, the office accommodation, mess rooms, toilets and locker rooms all had to be enlarged, and this was accomplished by add-on extensions to the existing facilities on the eastern wall of the main building. The stores had its capacity almost doubled, and this was achieved by double-decking over the existing floor area. Another improvement soon found necessary was to increase the capacity of the roof fume extractor fans, especially over No 1 road now that so many locomotives were passing through the shed for servicing, and with their engines running. Even after these improvements, to prevent fumes spreading to the remainder of the shed, a screen was erected between cant-rail level and the roof itself,

longitudinally between Nos 1 and 2 roads for the whole length of the shed; this effected a vast improvement for staff working at roof level on locomotives elsewhere in the depot.

A much earlier improvement was the strengthening of No 5 road at the northern end of the depot, so that a set of four Matterson 25-ton lifting jacks could be used, and these enabled a complete locomotive body to be removed from its bogies. The bogies could then be towed into one of the bays, then being under an overhead crane, so that traction motors and wheelsets could be changed. This happened in late 1963 or early 1964, and prior to this locomotives needing such attention had to go into Crewe Works. In 1963 the Workshops Division of BR had been formed, and this removed the main workshops from the control of the Regional Chief Mechanical & Electrical Engineers. A direct result of this was that depots had to think more about helping themselves, rather than proposing locomotives for attention in a main workshop. Before the installation of these jacks, the pony truck springs of the English Electric Type 4 diesels, with their massive 'Bulleid' 1-Co-Co-1 plate frame bogies, had to be changed by use of the wheeldrop at Crewe North. This was because it was impossible to jack the complete locomotive high enough with conventional jacks, to be able to get the springs out of position; they sat on top of the axle boxes, which were between the frames — the pony truck being allowed sideplay within the main bogie frame. This was a very dirty, and generally lousy job, and it was made much easier when the whole bogie could be removed from the locomotive.

Other improvements as the diesel fleet increased included an extension of this jacking facility, but before this could be undertaken other developments need to be described. In 1965, prior to the North Shed closing, additional facilities for steam locomotives had to be installed at the South Shed. Perhaps surprisingly, in view of its size and age, this depot had very largely relied on the North Shed to carry out the larger mileage examinations and repairs to its fleet. Even when it carried out such examinations itself, it relied on the machine shop at the North Shed to undertake all machining work such as bearing remetalling. Rather than move the (by this time quite old)

machinery from the North Shed and install it at the South Shed, the decision was taken — very logically — to use the almost new and virtually unused equipment from the Diesel Depot which was a legacy of the place having originally been designed for steam.

The result of this at the Diesel Depot, was a large open space between the bay roads at the south end of the shed and the substation. Therefore, Nos 6 and 7 roads were extended, without pits, into this space abutting the substation, giving room for two more locomotives. At the same time No 5 road, which had a section at its centre without a pit, was reconstructed with a pit for its entire length, and its southern end was strengthened like the north end so that a second set of Matterson jacks could be used. Thereafter two locomotives could be lifted separately on this road.

A new road-borne 6-ton crane was purchased, and it was intended that this could work in the former machine shop area, and provide additional overhead lifting capacity for locomotives stabled on the extended Nos 6 and 7 roads. However, despite adequate headroom, this practice did not last for long, and it was found that space to manoeuvre the crane was very limited. Nevertheless, this crane, and its successors, have been extremely useful, and a lot of lifting work is undertaken outside the depot at the northern end, where there already existed quite a large concrete apron which was extended to give the crane an even greater operating area.

Even further increases in the depot's workload resulted from the introduction of the Brush Type 4 (later Class 47) locomotives, and the final demise of steam with the arrival of the English Electric D400s (later Class 50). Yet further enlargement of the offices and staff amenities was necessary, and was again accomplished by grafting on extensions along the eastern wall of the main shed; much later still, in around 1976, a completely new administration building was constructed south of the shed. I have a note that D1633 was the first Brush Type 4 to have an examination at the Diesel Depot, a 125-150hr exam on 29 December 1964 — it had been new earlier that month and was, I believe, the first of its type to be allocated to Crewe North.

The North Holding Sidings remained in use after the final demise

**Above:**

**With the introduction of the summer timetable on 4 May 1970, the Anglo-Scottish workings north of Crewe were diagrammed for pairs of the English Electric Type 4 2,700hp D400 class in an attempt to speed up the service prior to the decision to electrify the line. Seen here on that day are Nos D437 and D447, standing on the Diesel Depot, and ready to work the down 'Royal Scot'. Alongside, from left to right can be seen Fitters Tony Hope, David Owen and Barry Harding. The whole class was allocated to Crewe when new, and the locomotives had been ordered specially to work to Anglo-Scottish traffic. They started to migrate in numbers to the Western Region on completion of electrification north of Crewe in 1974, although a few had been transferred earlier.** *Allan Baker*

**Left:**

**Crewe Diesel Depot on 4 May 1970, showing one of the pair of locomotives prepared to work the down 'Midland Scot', which was the earlier Glasgow departure from Crewe, having started its journey in Birmingham.** *Allan Baker*

**Top right:**

**Crewe North Holding Sidings, towards the end of their life in June 1970, with Class 50s No D443 and D442 awaiting their next turns of duty. The 1938-built Crewe North Junction Signalbox is behind.** *Leslie Riley*

**Right:**

**Class 37 No 37250 leaving the washing plant, situated in what had been the Down, or Old Yard, on 27 February 1988. This view looks south, and the newer fuel storage tanks can be seen to the left.** *Gavin Morrison*

of steam at Crewe, and this occurred with the closure of the South Shed to steam on and from Sunday 6 November 1967. Likewise diesels, especially shunting types, continued to be stabled at the South Shed, but fuelling there ceased, and all remaining maintenance staff were transferred to the Diesel Depot. Very soon after this, however, a scheme was developed to vacate the North and South Shed sites, insofar as locomotive stabling was concerned, and completely rationalise the facilities.

This scheme, in essence, entailed swapping the Old Yard with the South Shed, and it will be recalled that the former was the quite extensive yard alongside the Diesel Depot, and between it and the main lines; by this time it dealt mainly with parcels traffic. Obviously, if this yard could be remodelled and become locomotive holding sidings, there would no longer be any need to stable locomotives at either the North or South Shed sites, and this is what took place.

First of all, the South Shed site was cleared and then remodelled with 10 sidings, all converging at either end,

and a limited amount of overhead line equipment was installed; it then became the parcels marshalling yard for Crewe. Next, the Old Yard was almost completely cleared, and a new connection laid at its southern end, to provide connection with the up and down Shrewsbury lines; previously there had been no connection here. The scheme was that locomotives would enter the new yard at this point, under the control of the Gresty Lane No 1 signalman and then, before proceeding through a newly installed washing plant and on to an equally new fuelling point, a decision would be made if the locomotive needed to visit the depot itself. This could be for either a scheduled examination, an A exam, or some form of repair that could not be performed in the Holding Sidings. If it needed to visit the depot, it would proceed via the previously little-used connection between Old Yard and No 1 depot road, before changing direction and entering the depot.

Coincident with these new arrangements, which came into use on Monday 3 August 1970 at 06.00, the North Holding Sidings were taken out of use, and the area was soon

completely cleared. At the same time, the connection between the Diesel Depot yard and the independent lines was also taken out of use. This section, as we have seen, had been a perpetual cause of problems with bank slippage, and doubtless the Civil Engineer heaved a sigh of relief. It was of course rendered very largely superfluous by the new arrangements.

Above left:
**At the north end of the depot, on No 1 road, ScotRail Class 47/7 No 47706 *Strathclyde*, together with Class 47/4 No 47420 and Class 25 No 25063, await entry into the shed for servicing; notice the fuel storage tanks behind them. This photograph was taken on 1 June 1985, and the Class 47/7 would be at Crewe having recently been released from Crewe Works.** *Gavin Morrison*

Below:
**The south end of the Diesel Depot on 1 June 1985, and showing clearly the three roof sections, and the new office block to the right; on the extreme left is the run-round road. Locomotives visible, from left to right are: Nos 25202, 25298, 25297, 47234, 25229 and 25213. Crewe had large allocations of the various varieties of Sulzer Type 2s for much of their lives.** *Gavin Morrison*

Above right:
**Inside the depot on No 5 road north, Class 47/0 No 47355 is lifted for its bogies to receive attention; alongside on 27 February 1988 are Nos 47436 and 47433.** *Gavin Morrison*

Right:
**On the same date as the previous view, Class 47s Nos 47003 and 47350 *British Petroleum* stand alongside each other, respectively on Nos 6 and 7 bay roads at the south end of the depot; notice the 2½-ton overhead travelling crane above them. In the foreground is the area that was originally part of the machine shop.** *Gavin Morrison*

The new washing plant was not quite ready when the other facilities came into use, and was commissioned on 21 December 1970; it could wash a complete locomotive, except its ends, in a matter of minutes, and without the driver even having to get out of his cab.

The Diesel Depot lives on today, very largely unchanged, except for the removal of the life-expired Atlas wheel-turning lathe. This machine has not been replaced because newer, and faster machines installed elsewhere can encompass its workload. Removal of this machine presented the opportunity to construct a third jacking pad, and three locomotives can now be lifted from their bogies simultaneously. Over the

years the depot's allocation of locomotives has changed somewhat, and with the present policy of dedicating fleets of locomotives to particular traffics, Class 31/1s and 31/4s have joined the longer-term residents. The depot has a long-term future under the BRB's depot strategy, but will always be best remembered for its efforts with the English Electric Type 4s (Class 40s), and the infamous D400s (Class 50s). Ironically, Crewe Diesel Depot was the last home for the last Class 40, No 40122 — the erstwhile D200. With a reputation for considerable versatility, the depot has, over the years, turned little work away, and in the present business environment this can only enhance its reputation.

Below left:
**On the same date, but this time showing No 5 road south, with No 47598 lifted from its bogies, and two Class 20s on the adjacent road. The flexible hose on the bogie is being used to transmit hot air to a traction motor, in an attempt to lift its insulation valve.** *Gavin Morrison*

Below:
**An aerial view of the southern end of Crewe, showing the North Stafford line curving away from the main line in the top left-hand corner, the Carriage Shed between it and the main line, and the Diesel Depot in the centre. In the foreground can be seen the Independent lines, and Salop Goods Junction signalbox, with Basford Hall Marshalling Yards in the distance. The Shrewsbury line crosses over the Independent lines, and behind the Diesel Depot can be seen the Parcels Marshalling Yard, the former site of Crewe South Shed. The prefabricated building to the left, between the cutting and the locomotive holding sidings, is the Bungalow, and the site of the former connection between the Diesel Depot and the Independent lines can be seen below it: the date is 27 February 1988.** *Gavin Morrison*

# 8
# Electric Traction Depot

Under the LMR's plans to electrify the West Coast main line between Euston, Manchester and Liverpool, via both Crewe and the NSR route through Stoke-on-Trent, at 25kV ac, a line organisation of District Electric Traction Engineers (DETE) was set up. Unlike diesel traction, which had been managed from inception by the existing motive power structure, the new electric railway including the overhead line equipment and power distribution arrangements would be managed as a separate entity. DETEs were appointed, with support organisations, initially at Crewe, Manchester (Longsight) and Liverpool (Allerton) with later additions, as the electric railway spread, at Rugby and London (Willesden). Each was to be supported by, and be located at, a District Electric Traction Depot, and at these depots there were not only to be facilities for the maintenance and repair of the new rolling stock, but also the necessary workshop support and amenities for the overhead line and distribution repair and maintenance gangs too. The Electric Control Rooms were also to be located at the depots, and this was the case at Crewe, Rugby and Willesden. The area covered by the DETE Crewe was from Weaver Junction, Chelford and Macclesfield in the north, to Rugeley in the south. However, the Control Room supervised the entire electrified route to the north, and abutted the Rugby area at Rugeley to the south. The site chosen for the new depot at Crewe was part of that originally used for the carriage workshops, yard and storage sheds, south of the Chester line and one mile west of Crewe North Junction. Rail access to the site was available from both east and west, not only from the Crewe-Chester line, but also directly to the locomotive works, via the famous Eagle Bridge, and another bridge over the Carriage Works Yard. The first of these bridges took the single-track connecting line between the Works and Carriage Works Yard, over the Crewe-Chester line, before it joined the Steel Works Yard just west of the Deviation Works. It was in this area, by the Eagle Bridge, that the

original route of the line from Crewe to Chester joined the formation of the new direct line, opened on 27 July 1868, and thus allowed more room for the expansion of the Old Works, and the construction of the Deviation Works — hence its name. As we saw in an earlier chapter, this new line also encroached on part of the North Shed Yard.

Eagle Bridge gets its name from four rather fine cast iron eagles, one mounted on each of the buttress corners, and which are reputed to have arrived at the steel works in a consignment of scrap for melting at about the time the bridge was being built in 1870. Legend has it that they were seen as they were about to disappear in the furnaces by F. W. Webb himself, during one of his tours of inspection through the Melting Shop and that they took his fancy. He gave immediate orders that they be put to one side, and subsequently arranged for them to be mounted on the bridge as described. They sit on cast iron stands, bearing a capital letter 'C', which are integral with them and, therefore, one presumes of some significance to their origin; it has been suggested that they started life somewhere in Conway, but nobody seems to know for certain. Unfortunately, when this bridge was lifted to provide the necessary clearance for the overhead line equipment, the splendid eagles became even more difficult to see properly than they had been before, but since then they have been removed and relocated at the Crewe Heritage Centre, which was opened in 1987 to celebrate Crewe's 150-year involvement in railways. Whilst they can now be seen more clearly, it is a pity they have been removed from where they had rested for over 100 years.

The original coach construction and repair shops at Crewe were in the Old Works and later, to allow for the expansion of the activities there in connection with locomotives, they were moved east of the main line and into the apex of land between the Preston and Manchester lines; later still, in the late 1870s, completely new shops were built on the site currently

under review. Although it was the practice for all new carriage construction on the LNWR to be undertaken at Wolverton Works, the Crewe shops were responsible for a lot of the repair work. They closed in 1932, although the carriage storage sheds remained in use for some time longer. The site was later cleared and utilised for a new apprentice training school, which opened in 1955.

To the west of the Carriage Works were the cooling ponds (still in existence) for the Steel Works furnaces, which themselves closed on cessation of steelmaking at Crewe on 30 September 1932. Although the Carriage Works was allowed to fall into disrepair and was later demolished, the Steel Works remained intact, and was reopened under the direction of the Ministry of Supply, to assist the war effort in March 1941, only to close again — this time for good — in 1946. The Melting Shop itself, the highest of the Works buildings and known to one and all as 'The Melts', remains to this day, and is situated almost exactly on the opposite side of the Chester line to the Electric Traction Depot. As I pen these words, however, I believe its demolition is imminent.

The site of the Carriage Works Yard and the remainder of the storage sheds was cleared in the late 1950s, and used as an electrification construction depot, and it was in this area that the new District Electric Depot was built. Construction started in 1959, and the depot opened in stages, becoming available for locomotive and electric multiple-unit (EMU) maintenance in early 1960. The control room became fully operational on the inauguration of the electric service between Crewe and Manchester on 12 September 1960. There had also been a construction depot at East Didsbury on the Styal Loop Line between Wilmslow and Longsight, and as it was thereabouts that the first sections of overhead line equipment were energised; the early deliveries of electric locomotives were tested and commissioned there. Many of the original members of the DETE's Crewe team, who were the first staff for the organisation appointed, spent a lot of time at East Didsbury on this work, and the early driver training, and maintenance staff familiarisation, was undertaken there.

This is perhaps a good juncture to make mention of an interesting practice that dated from the closure of Stoke Locomotive Works in 1926. The majority of the displaced staff from Stoke were relocated in similar jobs at Crewe where much of the work had been transferred. Part of the agreement on their relocation was the provision of a special train service, in both directions, starting from the southern Pottery towns and running to Crewe. However, in view of the distance between the workshops in the Deviation and Steel Works from the station at Crewe, the train ran to a specially-built platform to the south of, and exactly opposite, the Carriage Works. From there, it was a short walking distance to either the Eagle Bridge for those heading towards the southern end of the Steel Works and the Deviation Works, and a footbridge over the Chester line almost alongside the new No 10 erecting shop, built in 1926, for those heading for the northern end of the site. Special arrangements were made for this train to run beyond the

Steel Works signalbox on the Chester line, and then propel into the Carriage Works Yard (and later the Electric Traction Depot) but on its return journey, it made direct access to the up Chester line, via the connection to the Yard nearest Crewe North Junction. By these different arrangements in the morning and evening, the number of facing points the train had to cross over was minimised and, therefore, the number that needed to be specially clipped for this passenger train movement was reduced. Latterly, this train sometimes found its way into the public timetables as far as Crewe, starting and finishing its journeys at Cresswell, 7½ miles south of Stoke, and it was the last train of the local Pottery services to be steam-hauled. During the day the coaching stock stood at a specially-built platform in the Electric Traction Depot Yard, but the service became a DMU in around 1970, and ceased to run completely in 1978. Although originally worked by Stoke engines and men, latterly it was a Crewe North job, with the engine taking the 03.55hrs Crewe to Longport newspapers, then running light to Stoke to turn, and continuing light to Cresswell before working the train to Crewe. Consequently, it became a

regular running-in turn for engines just ex-works, and many and varied was the motive power used. During the years I used this train I observed all the LMR passenger and mixed traffic locomotive types that were repaired at Crewe, except the ex-LMS Pacifics, along with most of the BR Standard types too, and including both 'Britannia' and 'Clan' Pacifics. I have even seen an ex-LNER B1, which had arrived at Crewe out of course and was being made use of, and on Bank Holidays when the Works was open, diesel types, including both the 'Warship' and 'Western' diesel

Below:
**A somewhat grimy Crewe North Class 5, is seen here leaving Harecastle North Tunnel with the Works train, which ran unadvertised between Crewe Works and the Stoke area specially for the staff; this dated from the 1926 closure of Stoke Works, and mention of it is made in this chapter. In the foreground can be seen clearance works under way in preparation for the deviation of the main line around Harecastle Middle and South Tunnels, as a part of the electrification of the route through North Staffordshire. The splitting home signals were for Kidsgrove Central Junction, where Crewe and Manchester lines divided. Photograph taken about 1964.** *Martin Welch*

hydraulics. It was interesting travelling to one's work in those days! Knowing many of the Crewe North men, I frequently managed to have a footplate ride, and it was on one of these workings that I first fired a main line steam locomotive, and got my first wet shirt.

The new Electric Traction Depot measured 300ft × 95ft, with the offices, workshops and other amenities occupying a two-storey block, integral with, and running the complete length of the depot to its southern side; this block is 75ft wide. Four roads pass through the depot, with access to all at either end, and each has a 270ft-long inspection pit, which dimension was derived from the length of a four-coach EMU of the type to be maintained there. Overhead line equipment passes through the shed on each road, and there are means of isolating and earthing each road separately, when it is necessary for staff to work on the roofs of vehicles, or otherwise need the supply switched off. There is a system of isolation, as near as foolproof as it is possible to get, to protect staff working in such circumstances.

The road nearest the amenity block has its overhead line equipment at the maximum off-centre stagger, 18in, thus allowing improved access to the roof equipment like the pantograph and air blast circuit breaker, should it be necessary to remove or refit these items with a crane. A mobile road crane is provided for this and other purposes, and there is ample room for it to manoeuvre in a specially large area between the pit and the dividing wall between depot and amenity block. This road is also strengthened to allow the use of two sets of four Matterson jacks, each jack with a 20-ton lifting capacity and almost identical to those used at the Diesel Depot, except the latter have an individual capacity of 25 tons. Thus two locomotives or EMU coach bodies can be lifted from their bogies simultaneously so that traction motors and wheelsets etc can be removed.

The depot was equipped to maintain around 80 main line electric locomotives and 40 EMUs, on their then maintenance cycles, but originally it was not the practice to allocate individual units to particular depots, although in actual fact vehicles did tend to keep going back to the same depots time and time again. Crewe generally became the home for the

Top:
**An early view inside the Electric Traction Depot, and before the construction works were complete. On No 1 road can be seen Class AL1 Bo-Bo locomotive No E3002; notice the Matterson lifting jacks, and overhead line equipment inside the building. This view looks south.**
*British Railways No DM6936*

Above:
**General view of the east end of the depot, showing the offices and administration block to the left, and Class 85 No 85024, on 27 February 1988.** *Gavin Morrison*

AL1 (later Class 81) and AL5 (later Class 85) Bo-Bo locomotives, and the AM4 (later Class 304) multiple-units; the latter being used on the local Crewe to Manchester and Liverpool services.

As the electrification extended towards London, and the use of steam traction reduced, along with the LMR's decision eventually to

separate locomotive maintenance completely from train crew management (forerunner of the Train Crew Concept, just coming to fruition now), the DETE's organisations were disbanded in April 1965. In their place the whole of the maintenance of diesel and electric traction was brought together under a series of Divisional Maintenance Engineers with support organisations and located at the headquarters of the local traffic divisions. In the case of Crewe this was at Stoke-on-Trent, and many a North Western man must have turned in his grave to see the mighty Crewe controlled from the headquarters of the little NSR! In its day, the LNWR had employed nearly as many men at Crewe as the NSR had employed on its entire system!

The plan was for train crew management, consisting of both footplatemen and guards, to be gradually transferred to the control of the area managers, and for locomotive carriage and wagon, electrification and plant and machinery maintenance to come under the control of what later became area maintenance engineers. These engineering managers were responsible to the Regional Chief Mechanical & Electrical Engineer (CM&EE) for maintenance standards, and the Divisional Manager for day-to-day operation of the railway. Usually, as by this time steam traction was well on its way out, the steam depots were left to be run locally under the existing organis-ations, consisting of shedmasters, having control of maintenance and footplatemen, and reporting to the Divisional Maintenance Engineer on maintenance aspects, and the Div-isional Operating Superintendent on operating matters. This was the case at Crewe South, but once that depot closed the train crews came under the control of the Area Manager. To accommodate these changes a new organisation was brought in with its headquarters at the Electric Traction Depot. This was initially under the control of a depot superintendent — later retitled Area Maintenance Engineer — who had control of that depot, the Diesel Depot and all the carriage and wagon and plant and machinery activities in the Crewe area, as well as the distribution of the overhead power supply, and the maintenance and repair of the over-head line equipment; indeed, all the

activities for which the Regional CM&EE was responsible.

The plant and machinery staff had been located in accommodation to the south of the North Shed, and between it and the Nantwich Road, and they were relocated at the Electric Traction Depot early in 1966. Later, this group became responsible for all the maintenance and repair of the civil engineers on-track plant (tampers, cranes, track layers and the like) and they undertook this work at the Electric Traction Depot. No 4 road — that farthest away from the amenity block — was generally reserved for this purpose. On closure of the Wagon Repair Shops at Crewe

Above:
**No 85024 again, this time inside the depot on No 3 road, with Class 81 No 81009 alongside, and Class 87/1 No 87101 *Stephenson* behind. This last locomotive is the only one of its kind, having solid state transformer tap changing, but otherwise being identical to the remainder of the class.**
*Gavin Morrison*

Below:
**The No 1 road in the depot — the Lifting Road — showing the Matterson jacks, and the road mobile crane. From left to right can be seen Class 85 Nos 85030, 85016 and Class 81 81012. Notice that ample space is available between No 1 road and the wall, to allow the road crane to manoeuvre: 27 February 1988.** *Gavin Morrison*

motives and rolling stock by BR has been a completely fresh look at Maintenance Depot Strategy, as a result of which it was announced that Crewe Electric Traction Depot will cease to maintain and repair locomotives and rolling stock after 1990 and its future thereafter would be in some doubt. However, recent 'fine tuning' of the plan, seems to give the depot an assured future under the dedicated locomotive fleet rules, as the 'home' of those electric locomotives belonging to the freight sector. But the amenity block does serve other purposes, not least the overhead line and distribution staff workshops, etc, and the Electric Control Room, and so its future in one form or another seems assured.

Gresty Lane, this work was transferred there in May 1983. This made room for work undertaken at Crewe on the Advanced Passenger Train during its development trials. Other than the changes just outlined, little has altered over the years at Crewe Electric Traction Depot. Until recently, it was the practice — because Crewe Works had no overhead line equipment — to remove pantographs and air blast circuit breakers from locomotives before they went into the Works for overhaul. Similarly, after repair at the depot they were refitted when the locomotives emerged again, and the commissioning was undertaken on the depot by depot staff. Under the BRB's new Manufacturing and Maintenance Policy, the bulk of the electric locomotive overhauls have been transferred from Crewe Works to Stratford Depot in London, and the few that still find their way to Crewe are fully commissioned by the Works, which now has the necessary facilities. As a part of the electrification of the main line from Crewe to Glasgow, completed in 1973, the Class 81 locomotives were transferred to Shields Depot in Glasgow for maintenance, and in 1987 the EMU fleet maintenance was moved to Longsight. Yet another aspect of the recent in-depth review of the maintenance and repair of loco-

Above left:
**Part of a 5-car Advanced Passenger Train (APT), seen at the north end of Platform 1 after a test run from Euston on 4 April 1985. A lot of the experimental work with these trains was undertaken with sets allocated to Crewe Electric Traction Depot, after abandonment of their concept for normal service use, but whilst much technical data was still being gathered. View looks north.** *L. A. Nixon*

Below:
**Brand-new Class 90 electric locomotive No 90001, inside the Depot on 27 February 1988, and flanked by Class 81 No 81012 to the left, and Class 85 No 85010 to the right.**
*Gavin Morrison*

# Bibliography

*Britain's New Railway*, O. S. Nock — Ian Allan 1966

*Crewe Locomotive Works & Its Men*, Brian Reed — David & Charles 1982

*A Pictorial Tribute To Crewe Works In The Age of Steam*, Edward Talbot — Oxford Publishing Co 1987

*LMS Engine Sheds, Vols 1 & 4*, Chris Hawkins & George Reeve — Wild Swan 1981 & 1984

*LMS Sheds in Camera*, John Hooper — Oxford Publishing Co 1983

*LNWR Miscellany, Vols 1 & 2*, Edward Talbot — Oxford Publishing Co 1978 & 1980

*The LNWR Recalled*, Edward Talbot — Oxford Publishing Co 1987

*The London & North Western Railway*, O. S. Nock — Ian Allan 1960

*Motive Power Organisation & Practice* — London Midland & Scottish Railway 1946

*Railway Steam Cranes*, J. S. Brownlee — Author; Glasgow 1973

*The Social & Economic Development of Crewe*, W. H. Chaloner — Manchester University Press 1950

*West Coast Joint Stock: A Register of*, R. M. Casserley & P. A. Millard — Historic Model Railway Society 1980

*Railway Magazine* — Various Issues

*Railway World* — Various Issues

*Stephenson Locomotive Society Journal* — Various Issues

*Trains Illustrated* — Various Issues

# Appendix 1
**Locomotive Allocations Crewe — combined list for North and South Sheds: September 1935**

653; 655; 674; 675; 695; 1115; 1116; 1119; 2390; 2391; 2392; 2393; 2394; 2859; 2887; 2890; 2968; 2969; 2970; 2981; 2983; 3412; 3479; 3571; 4377; 4450; 4451; 4452; 4453; 4454; 5019; 5049; 5051; 5070; 5071; 5072; 5073; 5074; 5081; 5082; 5083; 5084; 5085; 5086; 5087; 5091; 5148; 5149; 5150; 5151; 5152; 5153; 5154; 5155; 5156; 5163; 5165; 5166; 5167; 5173; 5174; 5175; 5176; 5177; 5178; 5179; 5180; 5181; 5182; 5183; 5184; 5185; 5186; 5231; 5282; 5284; 5285; 5288; 5290; 5291; 5293; 5295; 5296; 5297; 5298; 5299; 5373; 5385; 5391; 5575; 5576; 5582; 5583; 5589; 5590; 5591; 5592; 5594; 5595; 5597; 5598; 5599; 5600; 5601; 5602; 5604; 5606; 5631; 5632; 5633; 5634; 5635; 5637; 5642; 5645; 5646; 5791; 5908; 5927; 5957; 5962; 5975; 6013; 6102; 6118; 6119; 6120; 6122; 6123; 6124; 6125; 6126; 6133; 6134; 6148; 6149; 6150; 6151; 6152; 6153; 6154; 6160; 6210; 6211; 6605; 6711; 7192; 7362; 7414; 7416; 7444; 7445; 7591; 7595; 7606; 7608; 7609; 7611; 7612; 7614; 7615; 7616; 7647; 7657; 7658; 7681; 7887; 7946; 8006; 8007; 8295; 8347; 8350; 8352; 8511; 8707; 8753; 8792; 8831; 8833; 8904; 8909; 8931; 8951; 9008; 9022; 9135; 9149; 9203; 9229; 9231; 9232; 9234; 9241; 9242; 9243; 9245; 9246; 9247; 9249; 9266; 9274; 9275; 9276; 9278; 9384; 13085; 16606; 16607; 16673; 16679; 16690; 16693; 16696; 20008; 20022; 22901; 22911; 22912; 22971; 22978; 25603; 25612; 25627; 25631; 25637; 25640; 25641; 25642; 25648; 25662; 25700; 25728; 25730; 25744; 25753; 25796; 25803; 27651

Total: 239

# Appendix 2
**Locomotive Allocations Crewe: November 1945**

*Crewe North*
322; 471; 492; 659; 660; 1115; 1156; 1157; 1163; 1172; 2323; 2403; 2447; 2453; 2469; 2487; 2488; 2544; 2608; 4801; 4807; 4808; 4832; 4833; 4834; 4835; 4836; 4837; 4838; 4862; 4863; 4864; 4865; 4874; 4875; 4876; 4907; 4908; 4909; 5131; 5255; 5312; 5314; 5316; 5317; 5354; 5369; 5374; 5375; 5379; 5381; 5394; 5403; 5404; 5412; 5422; 5441; 5448; 5495; 5521; 5523; 5530; 5532; 5539; 5540; 5546; 5548; 5549; 5551; 5555; 5601; 5617; 5637; 5666; 5668; 5674; 5675; 5676; 5681; 5683; 5684; 5686; 5687; 5688; 5689; 5690; 5703; 5720; 5721; 5722; 5725; 5733; 6113; 6125; 6126; 6131; 6132; 6139; 6146; 6147; 6153; 6154; 6156; 6157; 6160; 6161; 6162; 6163; 6165; 6166; 6167; 6168; 6201; 6204; 6206; 6207; 6208; 6209; 6210; 6211; 6212; 6233; 6234; 6235; 6236; 6252; 6605; 6711; 6742

Total: 129

*Crewe South*
402; 405; 448; 2785; 2885; 2920; 2946; 2947; 2949; 2950; 2952; 2955; 2956; 2960; 2961; 2962; 2968; 2974; 2980; 2982; 2983; 3009; 3412; 3704; 4064; 4126; 4300; 4453; 4595; 5020; 5028; 5033; 5034; 5037; 5038; 5044; 5048; 5059; 5060; 5064; 5067; 5069; 5072; 5073; 5074; 5089; 5097; 5108; 5134; 5143; 5146; 5148; 5181; 5183; 5195; 5197; 5198; 5235; 5236; 5239; 5240; 5248; 5254; 5264; 5270; 5271; 5300; 5305; 5384; 7074; 7076; 7079; 7087; 7088; 7090; 7092; 7095; 7120; 7121; 7122; 7123; 7124; 7266; 7280; 7309; 7330; 7344; 7362; 7384; 7414; 7416; 7444; 7445; 7451; 7523; 7524; 7526; 7602; 7608; 7616; 7633; 7653; 7665; 7680; 7681; 8326; 8346; 8687; 8693; 8906; 9027; 9146; 9198; 9209; 9210; 9230; 9241; 9263; 9296; 9349; 9357; 9396; 9445; 22971; 22978; 28458; 28583; 28614

Total: Steam 115  Diesel 13

## Appendix 3
**Locomotive Allocations Crewe: November 1950**

*Crewe North*
40332; 40402; 40425; 40527; 40659;
40660; 40933; 41111; 41112; 41115;
41151; 41160; 41167; 41229; 41267;
44678; 44679; 44680; 44681; 44682;
44683; 44684; 44685; 44758; 44759;
44760; 44761; 44762; 44763; 44764;
44765; 44766; 44770; 44771; 45028;
45217; 45502; 45503; 45504; 45506;
45510; 45511; 45513; 45523; 45525;
45528; 45529; 45543; 45546; 45547;
45548; 45586; 45592; 45634; 45647;
45666; 45674; 45678; 45684; 45686;
45689; 45724; 45733; 45738; 46101;
46113; 46118; 46125; 46128; 46146;
46155; 46157; 46158; 46206; 46207;
46208; 46209; 46210; 46211; 46212;
46225; 46229; 46233; 46234; 46235;
46236; 46243; 46246; 46248; 46252;
46458; 46459; 46680; 58388; 58429

Total: 95

*Crewe South*
42773; 42785; 42810; 42811; 42815;
42856; 42930; 42936; 42943; 42947;
42950; 42952; 42955; 42956; 42968;
42972; 42980; 42983; 42984; 43189;
43207; 44125; 44300; 44301; 44386;
44452; 44495; 44708; 44807; 44832;
44834; 45006; 45013; 45030; 45038;
45044; 45048; 45060; 45067; 45073;
45093; 45108; 45131; 45134; 45148;
45185; 45189; 45195; 45198; 45239;
45240; 45254; 45270; 45271; 45294;
45300; 45301; 45369; 47266; 47280;
47330; 47344; 47384; 47414; 47431;
47450; 47523; 47524; 47526; 47590;
47595; 47608; 47633; 47661; 47670;
47680; 48248; 48249; 48250; 48251;
48252; 48253; 48255; 48256; 48257;
48259; 48260; 48261; 48262; 48263;
48286; 48287; 48288; 48289; 48290;
48291; 48292; 48294; 48295; 48296;
48297; 48757; 49210; 49230; 49407;
51204; 51221; 12000; 12001; 12002;
12033; 12034; 12035; 12036; 12037;
12049; 12050; 12051; 12052; 12053;
12054; 12055; 12078

Total: Steam 107 Diesel 16

## Appendix 4
**Locomotive Allocation Crewe: April 1956**

*Crewe North*
40332; 40413; 40447; 40456; 40659;
40660; 40926; 41060; 41160; 41167;
41229; 41901; 42321; 42566; 42955;
42961; 42963; 42964; 44679; 44680;
44682; 44683; 44684; 44685; 44758;
44759; 44760; 44761; 44762; 44763;
44764; 44765; 44766; 44807; 44840;
45000; 45002; 45003; 45033; 45150;
45235; 45240; 45254; 45282; 45300;
45301; 45373; 45390; 45402; 45434;
45446; 45503; 45507; 45528; 45529;
45548; 45556; 45586; 45591; 45603;
45604; 45617; 45625; 45630; 45634;
45643; 45674; 45678; 45684; 45703;
45721; 45726; 45736; 46102; 46106;
46118; 46119; 46125; 46127; 46128;
46129; 46134; 46137; 46138; 46148;
46150; 46155; 46156; 46159; 46163;
46166; 46167; 46200; 46201; 46203;
46206; 46209; 46210; 46212; 46225;
46233; 46234; 46235; 46243; 46246;
46248; 46249; 46252; 71000; 78030

Total: 110

*Crewe South*
42776; 42777; 42785; 42811; 42813;
42815; 42851; 42856; 42894; 42920;
42926; 42933; 42939; 42940; 42944;
42950; 42952; 42953; 42956; 42962;
42968; 42972; 42980; 42983; 42984;
43189; 43330; 43562; 44186; 44301;
44344; 44359; 44385; 44592; 44595;
44827; 44832; 44834; 45041; 45044;
45067; 45073; 45074; 45093; 45108;
45111; 45128; 45131; 45134; 45180;
45185; 45188; 45189; 45198; 45270;
45353; 45354; 45369; 45391; 45426;
47330; 47384; 47414; 47431; 47450;
47516; 47523; 47524; 47526; 47668;
47616; 47661; 47670; 47680; 48248;
48251; 48252; 48255; 48256; 48257;
48258; 48262; 48263; 48287; 48288;
48289; 48291; 48292; 48294; 48295;
48529; 48630; 48736; 48743; 49230;
49407; 49448; 49454; 51218; 58196;
58271; 12000; 12001; 12002; 12004;
12005; 12009; 12010; 12012; 12013;
12019; 12020; 12021; 12022; 12023;
12029; 12030; 12031; 12032; 13172;
13175; 13176

Total: Steam 101 Diesel 21

## Appendix 5
**Locomotive Allocations Crewe: November 1960**

*Crewe North*
41212; 41220; 41229; 42079; 42575;
42776; 42815; 42940; 42958; 42963;
42966; 42968; 44678; 44679; 44680;
44681; 44683; 44684; 44685; 44714;
44759; 44761; 44762; 44763; 44764;
44765; 44770; 44844; 44911; 45003;
45004; 45021; 45033; 45037; 45073;
45132; 45189; 45235; 45240; 45243;
45250; 45254; 45257; 45289; 45311;
45348; 45369; 45379; 45446; 45528;
45529; 45534; 45545; 45553; 45556;
45591; 45595; 45604; 45628; 45629;
45630; 45634; 45643; 45655; 45666;
45670; 45674; 45676; 45684; 45689;
45726; 45736; 45737; 46110; 46111;
46115; 46116; 46125; 46127; 46128;
46129; 46134; 46135; 46136; 46149;
46152; 46155; 46159; 46164; 46166;
46169; 46200; 46205; 46209; 46212;
46220; 46221; 46228; 46229; 46235;
46241; 46248; 46249; 46251; 46254;
46256; 71000; 78030; D3; D8; D9;
D68; D69; D220; D224; D227; D230;
D297; D298; D299; D300; D301;
D305; D306; D307

Total: Steam 108 Diesel 17

*Crewe South*
42944; 42948; 42949; 42952; 42955;
42956; 42959; 42961; 42962; 42964;
42972; 42975; 42979; 42980; 42983;
42984; 43464; 44301; 44592; 44713;
44832; 44834; 44868; 45000; 45001;
45002; 45045; 45048; 45067; 45074;
45128; 45130; 45142; 45148; 45149;
45198; 45248; 45270; 45291; 45298;
45248; 45270; 45291; 45299; 45300;
45391; 45403; 45494; 47280; 47310;
47338; 47348; 47354; 47384; 47391;
47395; 47397; 47400; 47414; 47431;
47445; 47450; 47467; 47482; 47516;
47523; 47524; 47525; 47529; 47601;
47608; 47661; 47664; 47677; 47680;
48085; 48252; 48255; 48257; 48262;
48292; 48294; 48297; 48423; 48502;
48516; 48548; 48626; 48630; 48633;
48655; 48659; 48692; 48693; 48729;
48734; 48743; 49158; 49407; D2221;
D2236; D3089; D3175; D3245; D3291;
D3292; D3367; D3583; D3584; D3763;
12000; 12001; 12005; 12009; 12010;
12011; 12020; 12021; 12025; 12031;
12032

Total: Steam 99 Diesel 22

## Appendix 6
### Locomotive Allocation Crewe Diesel Depot: December 1968

It should be noted that at this period, it was the practice of the LMR not to allocate individual diesel main line (DML) locomotives to depots, but rather to Divisions. Therefore, the DML locomotives listed below were allocated to the Stoke-on-Trent Division, coded D05, but as Crewe was the only depot in the division with the full facilities for their maintenance, it can be taken that to all intents and purposes the locomotives listed below were allocated there. There were no such inhibitions with the diesel shunters (DS) and those listed below were all allocated to Crewe, coded 5A, which code it assumed on the closure of Crewe North. Its current code is CD.

216/217/233/297/305/306/307/308/309/ 313/314/315/318/319/320/321/323/335/ 336/337/400-49/1616/1617/1618/1619/ 1620/1621/1622/1623/1624/1625/1626/ 1627/1632/1633/1634/1635/1747/1748/ 1749/1750/1751/1755/1756/1757/1805/ 1808/1809/1810/1811/1812/1813/1814/ 1815/1816/1817/1818/1819/1820/1822/ 1823/1837/1838/1839/1840/1842/1843/ 1844/1845/1846/1847/1848/1849/1850/ 1851/1852/1853/1854/1855/1856/1857/ 1953/1954/1955/1956/1957/1958/1959/ 1960/1961/1962/1963/1964/1965/1966/ 1967 5000-50/5051-66/5073-93/ 5133-42/5144/5145
2385/2386/2387/3006/3031/3032/3068/ 3083/3098/3105/3113/3181/3245/3247/ 3290/3291/3292/3462/3467/3471/3583/ 3763/3798/3799/3800/3801/3861/3870/ 3984/4108/4110/4111/4112/4114/4143
12047/12052/12055/12062/12066/ 12069/12082/12084/12091/12092/ 12093/12096

Totals: DML 235; DS 47  Grand Total: 282

## Appendix 7
### GWR Locomotive Allocation: Crewe January 1923

| No | Type | Class | Built | Withdrawn |
|---|---|---|---|---|
| 312 | 0-6-0 ic | 131 | Swindon No 47/1865 | 3/1923 |
| 1554 | 0-6-0ST ic | 1501 | Wolverhampton No 390/1880 | 1944 |
| 3218 | 2-4-0 ic | Barnum (3206) | Swindon No 1149/Oct 1889 | 11/1930 |
| 3237 | 2-4-0 ic | 3232 | Swindon No 1346/Oct 1892 | 3/1928 |
| 3308 | 4-4-0 ic | Bulldog | Swindon Rebuilt Jan/1909 | 8/1938 |
| Falmouth | | | | |
| 4312 | 2-6-0 oc | 4300 | Swindon No 2408/1911 | 11/1938 |
| 4383 | 2-6-0 oc | 4300 | Swindon No 2654/1916 | 3/1936 |

ic — inside cylinders
oc — outside cylinders

The dates of withdrawal do not necessarily indicate that the locomotives in question were still allocated to Crewe at the time.

## Appendix 8
### GWR Locomotive Allocation: Crewe 31 December 1947

Although Crewe was always a sub-shed of Wellington, and therefore in the Wolverhampton Stafford Road district, it was the practice of the GWR to keep particular locomotives working from sub-sheds for long periods, and therefore to show them as allocated there. This practice ceased on formation of BR, and thereafter no such allocations were shown for Crewe, though the practice of certain locomotives remaining on duties that kept them at sub-sheds continued.

4154, 5139, 3749

## Appendix 9
### Observations of Shed Visits
Locomotives Observed on Crewe North Shed: 20 April 1952

40332, 40448, 40646, 40659, 40660, 41220, 41226, 41229, 41230, 41324, 42814, 44063, 44478, 44678, 44679, 44681, 44685, 44741, 44762, 44765, 44810, 44835, 44874, 44909, 45052, 45070, 45106, 45372, 45404, 45422, 45529, 45535, 45553, 45570, 45587, 45592, 45631, 45632, 45634, 45669, 45674, 45689, 46106, 46107, 46110, 46125, 46134, 46141, 46151, 46161, 46200, 46208, 46210, 46211, 46223, 46235, 46237, 46243, 46245, 46246, 46248, 46680, 47445, 58426, 73021, 80034

Total: 66

Locomotives Observed on Crewe North Shed: 26 April 1953

40332, 40413, 40425, 40527, 40659, 40660, 41076, 41229, 41320, 42433, 42543, 42575, 42605, 42607, 42677, 42814, 42815, 43207, 44678, 44680, 44681, 44684, 44770, 44835, 44840, 44913, 45017, 45051, 45125, 45134, 45141, 45187, 45190, 45245, 45286, 45301, 45330, 45413, 45421, 45434, 45506, 45510, 45523, 45535, 45544, 45551, 45555, 45578, 45586, 45591, 45595, 45604, 45636, 45678, 46101, 46111, 46118, 46125, 46134, 46136, 46137, 46139, 46140, 46147, 46148, 46206, 46209, 46211, 46224, 46227, 46228, 46234, 46243, 46245, 46254, 46255, 46256, 46257, 49119, 70030, 73002, 75000

Total: 81

Locomotives Observed on Crewe North Shed: 29 April 1954

40332, 40419, 40447, 40659, 40934, 41229, 41320, 42316, 42440, 42568, 42595, 42608, 44678, 44679, 44685, 44732, 44756, 44766, 44807, 44840, 44868, 45065, 45144, 45190, 45283, 45300, 45301, 45333, 45374, 45381, 45430, 45434, 45504, 45508, 45513, 45514, 45529, 45532, 45535, 45540, 45549, 45595, 45623, 45678, 45684, 45736, 46101, 46104, 46127, 46128, 46137, 46138, 46139, 46142, 46151, 46162, 46163, 46166, 46206, 46210, 46212, 46225, 46233, 46235, 46238, 46243, 46244, 46252, 47330, 47526, 48252, 73013
Western Region 4178

Total: 73